D1289816

# THE NAGARATHARS OF SOUTH INDIA

*An Essay and a Bibliography on the Nagarathars in India and South-East Asia*

*Also by S. Chandrasekhar*

*Population and Law in India*, 2nd ed. (Madras: Macmillan, 1978).

*Ananda K. Coomaraswamy* (1877-1947) (Madras: Blackie, 1977).

*Abortion in a Crowded World: The Problem of Abortion with Special Reference to India*, Foreword by Professor Garrett Hardin (London: Allen and Unwin; Seattle: University of Washington Press, 1974).

*Infant Mortality, Population Growth and Family Planning in India*, 2nd ed. (London: Allen and Unwin, 1972. Chapel Hill: The University of North Carolina Press, 1975).

*India's Population: Facts, Problems and Policies*, 2nd ed. (Meerut, India: Meenakshi Prakashan, 1970).

*Asia's Population Problems* (London: Allen and Unwin, 1967; 2nd ed. West-port, Conn. Greenwood Press, 1977).

*Problems in Economic Development* (ed.) (Boston: D. C. Heath, 1967).

*American Aid and India's Economic Development* (London: Pall Mall Press; New York: Praeger, 1966), Third Printing.

*Red China: An Asian View* (New York: Praeger, 1964), Fifth printing.

*Communist China Today*, 3rd ed. (London: Asia Publishing House, 1964).

*A Decade of Mao's China* (ed.) (Bombay: The Perennial Press, 1962).

*China's Population: Census and Vital Statistics*, 2nd rev. ed. (Hong Kong: Hong Kong University Press, 1962; New York: Oxford University Press, 1962).

*A Report on South Indian Reading Habits* (Madras: Southern Languages Book Trust and Ford Foundation, 1960).

*Report on a Survey of Attitudes of Married Couples toward Family Planning in the City of Madras* (Madras: Government of Madras Press, 1958).

*Indians in South Africa: A Survey* (Madras: Indian Institute for Population Studies, 1957).

*Population and Planned Parenthood in India*, Forewords by Jawaharlal Nehru and Julian Huxley, 2nd rev. ed. (London: Allen and Unwin, 1956. New York: Macmillan, 1956).

*Hungry People and Empty Lands*, 3rd ed. (London: Allen and Unwin; New York: Macmillan, 1955).

*India's Population: Fact and Policy*, 2nd ed. (New York: John Day, 1946, 1950).

# THE NAGARATHARS OF SOUTH INDIA

*An Essay and a Bibliography on the Nagarathars in India and South-East Asia*

S. CHANDRASEKHAR

© S. Chandrasekhar 1980

**All rights reserved. No part of this publication may be reproduced or transmitted, in any form or by any means, without permission**

*First published 1980 by*
THE MACMILLAN COMPANY OF INDIA LIMITED
Madras Bombay Calcutta Delhi
Associated companies throughout the world

Published by S. G. Wasani for
The Macmillan Company of India Limited and printed by
T. K. Sengupta at Macmillan India Press, Madras 600 002

DS
432
.N38
C47
1980

DEDICATED TO
THE MEMORY OF

Rajah Sir Annamalai Chettiar (1881–1948), Dewan Bahadur M. RM. Ramaswamy Chettiar (1854–1918), M. CT. M. Chidambaram Chettiar (1908–1954), Dr. K. V. AL. RM. Alagappa Chettiar (1909–1957), Karumuttu Thiagaraja Chettiar (1893–1974), AL. AR. Vellayan Chettiar (Zamindar of Devakottai) (1880–1945), A. M. M. Murugappa Chettiar (1902–1965), Pandithamani M. Kathiresan Chettiar (1881–1953), Raya Chockalingam Chettiar (1891–1974), Dewan Bahadur Dharmabhushanam T. N. Muthiah Chettiar (1841–1921) and So. Murugappa (1893–1956).

# PREFACE

For some years I have been interested in the social and economic characteristics of the Nagarathar (Nattukkottai Chettiar) community in South India. When I became Vice-Chancellor of Annamalai University in South India, founded half a century ago by a remarkable Nagarathar businessman and philanthropist after whom the University is named, I had an exceptional opportunity to study the community.

The Nagarathars are widely known in India and South-East Asia. Though small in numbers they are highly influential. And yet no serious study of the community had been made. Hence I decided to undertake a social survey of the Nagarathars.

On reviewing the available material it was decided that the survey could be published in two volumes. The first (and present) volume would deal with all the bibliographical materials on the Nagarathars available in English in various libraries in India and selected South-East Asian countries with an introductory essay. (A companion volume listing all the bibliographical items available in the Tamil language, with a Tamil translation of the introductory essay will be published later.)

The second and more substantial volume will deal with the growth and composition of the Nagarathar population, their marriage, family and fertility patterns, and their internal and external migration. It will also deal with their economic activities, ranging from village moneylending to international banking and large-scale industrialization. It will include the community's pioneering contribution to the economic development of Burma, Ceylon, Malaysia, Singapore, etc., as well as its philanthropic activities.

The research work connected with the survey was partly funded by kind donations from the Raja Sir M. A. Muthiah Chettiar, Shri AL. CT. Chidambaram Chettiar (Chidambaram Charity Trust), the A. M. M. Charities Trust, Shri A. V. Thyagaraja, Shri L. CT. L. Palaniappa Chettiar—all of Madras, Shri E. M. Viswanathan Chettiar of Pattukkottai, the Nagarathar Sangam of Madurai (Shri L. Alagusundaram Chettiar), the Nagarathar staff members of the Annamalai University, Shri Singaram Chettiar and his business colleagues in Chidambaram.

In the collection of bibliographic and other material on the Nagarathars I have been assisted by many persons—Nagarathars and others—in India and abroad too numerous to mention.

However, I would like specially to thank Messrs ST. Sethu, RM. Subbiah, N. M. Nagappan, Tan Sri M. S. Sundaram, Palaniappa Chettiar of the All-Malaysian Nattukottai Chettiar Endowment, S. Singaravelu and S. V. A. Annamalai Chettiar for their kind help during my visits to Malaysia.

In Sri Lanka, Dr. W. S. Weerasooria and Messrs R. M. Kasi Viswanathan Chettiar, K. V. S. Vyas and Dr. Dharma Thirunavukkarasu have been most helpful, and Mr. K. R. Veerappan in Singapore.

At the Annamalai University Messrs L. B. Venkatarangan, A. Shanmugam, S. Ranganadha, S. Thirugnana-sambandam and V. Durairajan rendered valuable assistance, as did our five Research Scholars, Misses M. Valliammal, AR. Geetha, M. Sivakami, Mrs. Meenakshi Narayanan and Mrs. Radha Lakshmanan.

Outside the campus, I am indebted to Messrs K. Nagarajan, Dr. V. SP. Manickam, Dr. M. Sundaram, Dr. SP. Annamalai, M. V. Arunachalam, Pulavar Naga Shanmugam, K. G. Krishnan and AR. Ramaswamy for information. Mr. A. V. Thiagaraja took more than an ordinary interest in the entire study.

Miss K. Dharmambal, Messrs R. Subramanian and Edwin Samuel shared the burden of typing notes, correspondence and the manuscripts.

Last, but hardly least, I am beholden to my wife for perusing this study and seeing it through the press.

Some material from the Introductory essay and the forthcoming second volume were presented as three All-Malaya Nattukkottai Chettiar Endowment Fund Memorial Lectures at the University of Malaya, Kuala Lumpur, in August 1978. In this connection my thanks are due to the Nagarathars of the Endowment Fund committee and Dr. S. Singaravelu and Professors Mohd. Taib Bin Osman, Yip Yat Hoong and Tunku Shamsul Bahrin of the University of Malaya.

Kodaikanal, South India<br>15 December 1978

S. CHANDRASEKHAR

# CONTENTS



## TABLES



## MAP

# INTRODUCTION

## I

## THE GEOGRAPHICAL SETTING: THE NATION, THE STATE AND THE DISTRICT

### 1. The Nation

Located on a vast ' tongue-shaped promontory that juts southwards from the continent of Asia ', India is well marked off from the rest of Asia by mountains and seas, stamping the country with an undeniable geographical unity as well as cultural isolation.

The country is bounded by the snow-capped Himalayas in the north, and tapering southward, by the Bay of Bengal on the south-east and the Arabian Sea on the south-west. On the east a series of mountain ranges separates India from independent Burma, which was once a province of the Indian empire under the British rule. (The then province of Burma, as we shall note later in our survey, plays an important part in the Nagarathars' overseas business operations.) To the east also lies independent Bangladesh, which came into existence as a new nation in December 1971 from its former position as the province of East Pakistan by seceding from the State of Pakistan, which is surrounded by the Indian territories of West Bengal, Assam, Meghalaya and Tripura. On the north-east, besides independent Nepal, lie the State of Sikkim, which is now politically integrated into India as a new State, and Bhutan, attached to India by a special treaty and as such considered a part of India. The independent nations of Pakistan (the former West Pakistan province) and Afghanistan border India on the north-west. In the south, the gulf of Mannar and the Palk Strait separate India from independent Sri Lanka (Ceylon). (The former British Ceylon also plays, as we shall note later in our survey, an important role in the overseas operations of the Nagarathars.) The Andaman and Nicobar Islands in the Bay of Bengal and Lakshadweep Islands (the Laccadive, Minicoy and Amindivi Islands) in the Arabian Sea are part of India's territory.

India has a land frontier 9,425 miles (15,200 km) long — actually a bit longer than the earth's diameter — and a coastline of 3,535 miles (6,083 km) which is roughly the distance from the Atlantic to the Pacific coast of the United States of America.

With an area of 1.2 million square miles (3,280,483 sq. km) India is about a third of the area of the continental United States of America excluding Alaska. India stretches about 2,000 miles (3,218 km) from Kashmir in the north to Cape Comorin or Kanyakumari in the south and about 1,850 miles (2,977 km) from Kutch in Gujarat in the west to Kohima in Assam in the east. The country lies entirely in the northern hemisphere and extends between latitudes 8° and 37° and longitudes 68° and 97°.

In the world, India is the second most populous and seventh largest country in area. The People's Republic of China with a 1978 estimated population of more than 900 million is the world's most populous nation; in area the first six largest nations are the Soviet Union, Canada, Peoples Republic of China, Brazil, the United States of America and Australia. The country's population in mid-1978 was estimated to have passed the 630 million mark, while its area, as already pointed out, is 1.2 million square miles.

## 2. The State: Tamil Nadu (Madras State)

The country, constitutionally a federal republic, is divided for administrative and other purposes into twenty-two states, roughly on the basis of the language spoken by the people. The evolution of the boundaries of these states from the pre-British and British times down to the linguistic reorganization of the Indian map by the Government of India in 1956 is a fascinating subject but it need not detain us here.[1]

In most countries of the world, the south is often considerably different from the north and has a culture and personality of its own, and India is no exception to this rule. This cultural differen-

[1]S. Chandrasekhar, 'The New Map of India', *Population Review* (Madras), January 1957, Vol. I, No. 1.

tial is generally a product of ethnic, linguistic and climatic differences. While waves of foreign invasions have shaken and shaped the north and some invaders even took near permanent shelter there, the south, by and large, has been unaffected by foreign intruders. Although it is true that the last of the invaders, the Europeans who came by sea, started at Madras in 1639, most of the other alien groups never reached the south or, when they did, were nearly a spent force. This fortunate historical circumstance has led to a remarkable degree of political stability and cultural continuity in the evolution of a distinct and distinguished culture and polity in South India which may be generically described as Dravidian.

And of these four Dravidian South Indian States (Kerala, Karnataka, Tamil Nadu and Andhra Pradesh), Madras State, or, to give its modern linguistic title, Tamil Nadu (literally, land of Tamils), is preeminently the cultural and linguistic heart and soul of Dravidian South India.

Of the four distinct southern languages, Telugu, Kannada, Tamil and Malayalam — constituting the Dravidian family of languages — Tamil is the Dravidian language *par excellence*, for it has the least link with such a northern Indo-Aryan language as Hindi and has a more ancient and renowned record of sacred and secular literature than the other three. (Some scholars believe that Tamil as a language is more ancient than Sanskrit, and is the mother of most of India's languages currently in vogue.)

Thus India has two major cultures — the Northern and Southern, the Indo-Aryan and Indo-Dravidian — with distinct modes of apparel and diet, a somewhat different social structure, and a definite general overall difference in life-styles.

Present-day Tamil Nadu has evolved from the sprawling Madras Presidency of the benighted British days which stretched from Malabar (which Malayalam-speaking district is now part of Kerala State) to Orissa (which is now a separate Oriya-speaking State on its own). The Madras Presidency lost first Orissa, and later, Andhra Pradesh was carved from it, leaving the fifteen largely Tamil-speaking districts to become Tamil Nadu including a little area, Kanyakumari and Nagercoil, carved out of the old princely State of Travancore which is now part of Kerala.

Tamil Nadu has an area of 50,490 square miles (130,069 sq. km), roughly the size of England in Great Britain or the State of New York in the United States. According to the 1971 census the State's population was 41.2 million and the 1976 mid-year estimated population was about 44 million. The State is divided for administrative purposes into fifteen districts which in turn are divided into *taluks* (minor administrative divisions).

The original and traditional home of the present Nagarathars is called Chettinad (or the land of Chettis, ' nad ' being an anglicised form of the Tamil word ' nadu ' meaning land or territory).[2] According to traditional sources based both on temple inscriptions and references in literature, the area of Chettinad is described as lying south of the Vellar river (the traditional boundary between the ancient Tamil Chola and Pandyan Kingdoms), north of the Vaigai river, east of the Piranmalai (or Parambu hill) a peak of only 1,800 feet above sea level, and west of the sea (the Bay of Bengal).

### 3. Ramanathapuram and Pudukkottai Districts

According to tradition, which is not without some historical

[2]The lack of standardisation of the spelling of Indian names in English is both remarkable and unfortunate. It is in a state of utter confusion. When the States (Provinces) of the Indian Union were reorganised on the basis of language, the old Madras Presidency of the British Raj was bifurcated into the Telugu speaking northern part, named Andhra Pradesh, land of the Andhras, and the southern part, Tamil Nadu, land of the Tamils. It would have been better if the world-renowned name Madras had been left to designate the residual State but some minor politicians could not think of any greater or more serious reforms than mere change of name.

And here again there was confusion, lack of euphony and uniformity. Tamil Nad as one or two words would have sounded better but the powers that be who were no linguists insisted on the English rendering being the exact equivalent of the Tamil term, and hence Tamil Nadu. And here again there was no standardisation; for even officially the name is written as one or two words. On the other hand, as we shall see later, the name Chettinad is written as one word and without ' u ' at the end. We shall therefore follow throughout the essay Tamil Nadu and Chettinad.

I have spelt Indian names—particularly jaw-breaking Tamil ones—with a minimum of diacritical symbols and in a manner which appeals to common sense.

supporting evidence, the Nagarathars migrated from Kaveri-poompattinam, the capital of the earlier Chola Kings (third century B.C. –second century A.D.) to what is now Chettinad. The original home, during the eighteenth century, consisted of some 96 villages. During the last two centuries Nagarathars from some of these villages have migrated to other parts of South India and to certain countries in South-East Asia in search of business opportunities. As a result, the Nagarathars are now distributed among some 78 villages — 58 of which are in the present-day Ramanathapuram[3] (the old Ramnad) district and 20 in the present Pudukkottai (the old small princely state) district.

## 4. Chettinad and its Villages

Chettinad, with an area of 656.7 sq. miles (1,700 sq. km), the original and traditional home of the Nagarathars, as already pointed out, is largely in the Ramnad district, on the Coromandel or Madras coast or within reach of it.

Historically, Chettinad is the name given to the original 96 villages of the Devakottah revenue division of Ramnad district and the Pudukkottah revenue division of Trichinopoly district.

The villages of present Chettinad are spread over four taluks, Tirupattur, Sivaganga and Thiruvadanai taluks in Ramnad district and Tirumayam Taluk in Pudukkottai district.

[3]Most of the names of the districts in Tamil Nadu have also been changed by the State Government into their proper Tamil names from the old anglicised names given by the British administration. Thus Ramnad has become Ramanathapuram, Trichinopoly has been changed to Tiruchirapalli, Madura to Madurai, Pudukkottah to Pudukkottai, etc. Several atlases prepared abroad still carry the old names. For the sake of quick identification the old anglicised forms are often used here.

## TABLE 1

### A List of Nagarthar Villages in Tamil Nadu†

1. Alagapuri (Kottaiyur)
2. Alavakottai
3. Amaravathipudur
4. Aranmanai Siruvayal
5. Arimalam
6. Ariyakudi
7. Athikkadu Thekkur
8. Attangudi
9. Attangudi Muthupattinam*
10. Avanipatti
11. Chockalingam-Pudur (Chockanendal)
12. Chockanathapuram
13. Devakottai
14. Kaliarmangalam
15. Kallal
16. Kalluppatti
17. Kanadukathan
18. Kandanur
19. Kandavarayanpatti
20. Kandaramanickam
21. Karaikudi
22. Karunkulam
23. Kilapungudi
24. Kilasivalpatti (& P. Alagapuri)
25. Kollangudi Alagapuri
26. Konapet
27. Koppanapatti
28. Kothamangalam
29. Kottaiyur
30. Kulipirai
31. Kuruvikondanpatti
32. Lakshmipuram (Kothamangalam) Lakshmipuram)
33. Madagupatti (Chockalingapuram)
34. Mahibalanpatti
35. Managiri
36. Melasivapuri
37. Mithalaipatti
38. Nachandupatti
39. Nachiarpuram
40. Natarajapuram*
41. Nattarasankottai
42. Nemathanpatti
43. Nerkuppai
44. Okkur
45. Oyakondan Siruvayal
46. Paganeri
47. Palavangudi
48. Pallathur
49. Panangudi
50. Panayappatti
51. Pariamaruthupatti
52. Pattamangalam
53. Pilayarpatti
54. Ponnamaravathy
55. Pulankurichi
56. Puduppatti (Ponnamaravathy)
57. Puduvayal
58. Ramachandrapuram
59. Rangiam
60. Rajavaram
61. Sakkandi
62. Sekkalai (Karaikudi)
63. Sembanur
64. Sevvur
65. Shanmuganathapuram (Aravayal)
66. Siravayal
67. Sirukudalpatti
68. Solapuram
69. Thanichavurani*
70. Thenipatti
71. Ulagampatti
72. Valayapatti
73. Vegupatti
74. Vendhanpatti
75. Vethiyur
76. Virachilai
77. Viramathi* (Kilasivalpatti)
78. V. Lakshmipuram (Virachilai)

†The villages are listed in alphabetical order.
The spelling used by the Posts and Telegrphs Department is followed herein.
*This symbol denotes places having no Post Offices.
Words within parentheses are alternate names used locally.

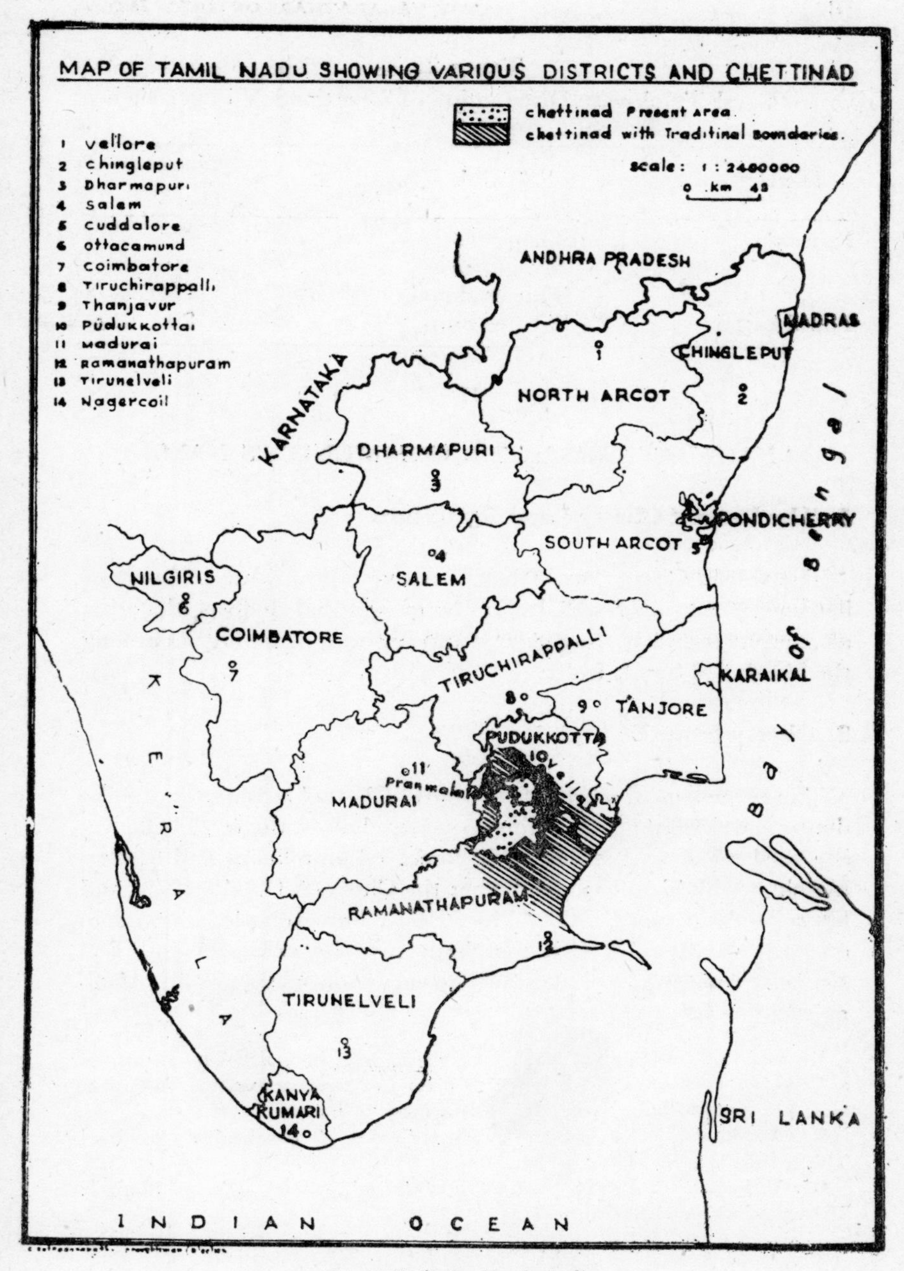


Tamil Nadu in South India

TABLE 2
District and Taluk-wise Distribution of Chettinad Villages Today

| District | Taluk | No. of Villages |
|---|---|---|
| Ramnad | Tirupattur | 45 |
| | Sivaganga | 10 |
| | Thiruvadanai | 3 |
| Pudukkottai | Tirumayam | 20 |

II

## 'NAGARATHARS': THE COMMUNITY'S NAME

### 1. The Term 'Chetty' and its Origin

The word 'Chetty' or 'Chetti' is a very general term, more or less common to all South Indian languages and dialects, denoting all merchant and trading groups and business communities among the Hindus of South India.

### 2. Chetty from Etti

The etymological origin of the word 'Chetty' is a matter of some doubt and dispute. According to some scholars, the term 'Chetti' is traced to 'Etti',[4] an honorific conferred on affluent and leading merchants by Tamil rulers during the Chola (A.D. 846–1279) and later Pandyan times (A.D. 1190–1310). For example, we read of one Etti Sayalan, a rich merchant in *Silappadikaram*[5] and Etti Kumaran, also a merchant of Kaveri-poom-pattinam in *Manimegalai.*[6]

[4]In ancient Tamil country leading merchants were honoured with such titles as 'Etti' by royalty. Etti is a flowering plant and garlands made of etti flowers were presented to affluent merchants as a mark of honour.

[5]U. V. Saminatha Ayyar (ed.), *Silappadikaram of Ilangovadigal* (Madras: Thiyagaraja Vilasam, 1955), p. 395.

[6]U. V. Samanitha Ayyar (ed.), *Manimekalai of Seethalai Sathanar* (Madras: Thiyagaraja Vilasam, 1956), p. 47.

It is believed that in the earlier centuries the local traders in the Tamil country were called ' Sattu ' and the overseas ones ' Nayagars '. And those businessmen who were successful enough in both internal and external trade to amass a fortune were honoured with the title ' Etti '. It is probable that the word ' Etti ' evolved in the course of a few centuries into ' Chetti '.

### 3. Chetty from Chettu

A second view is that the word ' Chetti ' is derived from the ancient Tamil word ' Chettee ' or ' Chettu ' which means a margin of profit earned in business. Some believe that the word ' Chetty ' is derived from the Tamil word *chikkanam* which means frugality or without waste. The word also connotes frugal habits, a sense of thrift and a life characterised by overall economy and careful management of money. Since the Chetty community today, despite great public generosity and lavish expenditure on such social occasions as weddings, leads a frugal, economic and even an austere life in private, it is thought that the genesis of the word must be traced to this particular parsimonious aspect of their domestic life. This view also derives some support from the fact that even today some merchants in North India are called ' Settus '. Akin to this is the fact that ' Chetty ' can also be derived from the near-archaic Tamil word *settirai* which is a form of customs duty or import tax, and hence ' Chettis ' derivatively as businessmen and traders.

### 4. Chetty from Shreshti

The third view is that the term is derived from the Sanskrit word *shreshti*. The root of the Sanskrit term *shresta* means important or superior, and it has even come down to this day as a proper surname as, Mr. Kula-Shreshta (meaning prominent family or one belonging to such a family). Jawaharlal Nehru, writing in a different context, points out, 'The Chettys of Madras have also been leaders in business and banking, especially from ancient times. The word " Chetty " is derived from the Sanskrit "Shreshti", leader of a merchant guild. The common appellation "Seth" is also derived from " Shreshti ". The Madras Chettys have not only played an important part in

South India, but they have spread out all over Burma, even in the remote villages.'[7] Thus 'Chetty' in the South and 'Seth' (or 'Sethji', a common denominator for rich merchants) in North India are popularly held to be derived from the Sanskrit, 'Shreshta', meaning great or prominent.

While these views may not be devoid of validity, the word might have been actually derived from *sreshti* which in Sanskrit simply means 'merchant'. We come across this term in several Sanskrit classics like *Atharva Samhitha* (I.9.3), *Satapatha Brahamana* (13.7.1.1) and *Aitareya Brahmana* (III. 30.3).

In the Pali literature, the Buddhist *Jataka*[8] tales, composed roughly about the fifth century B.C., we come across not only the term 'Shreshta' but such other terms as 'Setti' (member of a merchant guild), 'Maha-setti' (head of the guild), 'Anu-Setti' (assistant in the guild) and 'Uttara-Setti' (secretary to the guild), etc. The 'Settis' of the period were obviously engaged in trade and commerce and the criteria for the various sub-sects or sub-castes which apparently had already come into existence were possibly wealth, area of residence, or the official position in the trade guilds beginning roughly from the Mauryan period (325 B.C.–188 B.C.) of India's history.

As observed already, today in North India the term 'Sethji' is a common denominator for rich merchants, while in South India particularly in Mysore (the present Karnataka State), a dominant section of the merchant caste or the Vaishya community is called 'Shetty'.

## 5. Chetty and Chettiar

While the terms 'Chetty' or 'Chetti' are used as caste names at the end of given (proper) names as a mark of membership of a particular caste group, a further suffix 'ar' as an honorific or form of respectability has been added among the Tamil speakers during the last half a century; thus 'Chetty' becomes 'Chettiar'. For example, in the early decades of this century a prominent politician of South India was and is referred to as Sir P. T. Thyagaraya Chetty,

[7]Jawaharlal Nehru, *Discovery of India* (New York: John Day, 1950), p. 351.
[8]*Jataka,* I. 93, 120, 122; II. 319-20, 335; III. 49; IV. 38; V. 384; VI. 348.

and in recent times a distinguished South Indian politican and the first Minister for Finance in independent India as Sir R. K. Shanmukham Chetty; but today the leader of the Nagarathar community is referred to as Sir M. A. Muthiah Chettiar. (Thus, Mr. Ramaswami *Chetty* becomes Mr. Ramaswami *Chettiar* or simply Mr. *Chettiar.*)

Among the Telugu-speaking sub-caste, the honorific 'garu' (instead of Tamil *ar*) is added as a separate word, and thus 'Chetty garu', etc. However, the sub-caste community is simply referred to as 'Chettiars' as a genus.

Whatever may be the real origin of the word 'Chetty' or 'Chettiars', the present business-cum-banking community is subdivided into numerous sub-castes in Tamil Nadu.[9]

## 6. Nattukkottai Chettiar

However, the most enterprising, prominent and successful of these business and merchant sub-caste Chettiar groups is the Nattukkottai Chettiars or the Nagarathars.[10] How this particular sub-caste acquired these two names is an interesting indication of and a commentary on their economic milieu. The former (Nattukkottai Chettiar) name must be of relatively recent origin, for it refers to their affluence which dates, in its external manifestation, from the beginning of this century, when their financial operations overseas, particularly in Burma, proved a great success. Those Chettiars who amassed a fortune as a result of their business enterprise in Burma built huge homes, more or less mansions indigenous in style, in their ancestral villages in the Ramnad district of Tamil Nadu. Hence the name *Nattu-Kottai*, for these mansions, which literally mean 'country forts'. Thus *Nattu-Kottai* Chettiars or Chettiars who live in country forts or elegant country homes. It is intersting to note that the affluent Nagarathars, when they made their great fortunes at the turn of the century, did not give up their

[9]The Chettiars are sub-divided into such sub-castes as Arya, Vaisya, Beri, Devanga, Vania, etc.

[10]The Nattukkottai Chettiars are variously called Nagarthars, Nattukkottaiyar, Dhanavanigar, Dhanavaisyar, Nattarasankottai Chettiar, Chetti-Pillaigal, Dhani-desigal, etc.

ancestral villages, as might have been expected, and migrate to nearby urban areas in Madras, Madurai or Tiruchirapalli to build their mansions, but chose to remain in their traditional moorings.

## 7. The Nagarathars

The other name Nagarathars,[11] which is shorter, sounds better and which the present writer prefers, can be derived in three ways. *Nagaram* in ancient Tamil usage means a trading post or village. In the Chola period of South Indian history (A.D. 846–A.D. 1279) the term referred to a caste guild devoted to mercantile interests; and therefore *Nagarathars* simply means those who belong to a trading community.

Secondly, the word can also be derived from the Sanskrit root *Nagaraka*[12] or literally a city-dweller, or metaphorically one who is polished and urbane.

Yet another source for deriving the meaning of 'Nagarathar' is old Tamil literature. Therein *nagar* means palatial or spacious home. Hence Nagarathars mean those who are in the habit of building and living in large and commodious homes.

No matter what the philology and in which meandering way the name came about, we shall use the term *Nagarathars* throughout this study. And by it we mean the *Nattukottai* Chettiars, the Tamil-speaking business community belonging to the Hindu Saivite sub-sect of the Vaishya caste in the State of Tamil Nadu in India.

[11]'The Chettiars are called Nagarthars from the fact that they are grouped for social purposes into nine *Nagarams* or townships. At the head of each of these townships there is one temple . . . . Their population according to the 1921 census was 40,500 and the caste is divided into twenty-five "gotras" for purposes of marriage and adoption.' B. V. N. Naidu, 'The Nattukottai Chettiars and their Banking System', *Rajah Sir Annamalai Chettiar Commemoration Volume* (Annamalai University, India 1941), p. 457.

[12]See K. M. Panikkar's Introduction to *Kama Sutra of Vatsyayana* translated by Sir Richard Burton and F. F. Arbuthnot, (ed.) W. G. Archer (London: George Allen and Unwin, 1963).

## III

## THE NAGARATHAR COMMUNITY

Of the various communities in India based on caste, sub-caste, religion, religious sub-sect, language, dialect, regional or cultural groups, the Nagarathars are of unique interest for a variety of reasons to the social scientist.

Their total number, estimated to be about 100,000 is not known exactly. After the 1931 census of India, the question regarding the caste affiliation of citizens was dropped and since then it has been difficult to determine the exact numerical strength of any caste or sub-caste group in India.

But the pattern of their population distribution is fairly well documented because of their business enterprises, which are distributed all over Tamil Nadu (though their homeland is confined to Ramanathapuram and Pudukkottai districts) as well as overseas. While a great majority of India's population is described by successive Census Reports as ' stay-at-home ', bound to the homes and villages of the caste-cultural groups in which they are born and where they continue to live, the Nagarathars are one of the few enterprising communities (like the Sikhs and the Sindhis of the North) who have emigrated to such countries as Burma (Burma was a province of India till 1935), Ceylon, Singapore, Malaysia, Indo-China (present-day Vietnam and Cambodia), Indonesia and Mauritius. In these areas the Nagarathars established themselves during the last century and a half as prosperous and successful immigrant business groups.

From a demographic point of view the community is of considerable interest. From some fragmentary and inconclusive evidence, it is found that the Nagarathars are one of the few communities in India not experiencing the current population explosion which the nation's population as a whole has undergone during the last quarter century and more. This hypothesis about the community's low birth rate and consequent average small family size needs to be checked on the basis of a field study enquiring into the fertility pattern of Nagarathar families. The question is whether the small family norm of the Nagarathar is a reality, and, if so, the methods by which the community has been able to achieve this end.[13]

Another demographic aspect that requires exploration is the community's sex ratio. While the All-India population has exhibited over successive census decades an adverse sex ratio (930 females per 1000 males for India and 978 females per 1000 males in Tamil Nadu State in 1971) resulting in excessive masculinity and male dominance, this community's sex ratio seems to show a paucity of males and female domination. Indirect evidence on this subject indicates not only considerable anxiety on the part of many parents for male children but also a high rate of adoption of sons from eligible parents by affluent families with no male children of their own.

Secondly, from the sociological point of view, the community is of considerable interest. As we shall see presently, while no proper history of the Nagarathars based on authentic and reliable data has been written, both legend and tradition aver that the community is an ancient one and that the merchant Kovalan, the hero of the Tamil classic *Silappadikaram* (circa second century A.D.), authored by the Chera Prince Ilango Adigal, belonged to the Nagarathar community. It well might be.

Another feature of a sociological nature may be touched upon here. India, with her numerous religions, all the way from Animism to Zoroastrianism, and her wealth of religious experience both of a conformist and deviant nature, presents a veritable museum for the student of the sociology of religion. This subject, which has received so much attention in such apparently secular states as the United States of America, the United Kingdom and Germany, has as yet, for some strange reason, received scant attention in our country.

[13]The reasons behind the apparent low birth rate of the Nagarthar community are not clear. To begin with, the pattern of their traditional occupation from the early times—that is two centuries ago—has been for the adult male members to emigrate to countries of South-East Asia, leaving behind their wives and children, and return to them once in about three years. This forced separation no doubt contributes to their low birth rate.

The second reason may be, according to some geneticists, a function of their in-breeding. Before this factor can be accepted, one has to enquire into the merits of the question whether in-breeding leads to quasi-sterility. The theoretical evidence is not conclusive.

A socio-cultural indicator of the emotional and religious integration of a traditional religious community is the proportion of the community which opts for an alien and different faith. The lesser the percentage, the greater the integration. Though the Nagarathars and Nadars, for example, have co-existed for centuries in the same geographical area, very few Nagarathars have left Hindu Saivism, while many thousands of Nadars have embraced both Catholic and Protestant denominations of Christianity. The first thing the Nagarathars do on settling in a new area (whether in Tamil Nadu or in a foreign country) is to build a Saivite temple, and the ecology of the temple embraces many cultural, economic and social functions beyond those of a house of individual and communal worship. This is indicative of their intense religious loyalty as well as integration.

As for the community's economic activities, from their ancient occupation of selling and trading in salt, the Nagarathars became small village moneylenders many centuries ago. From simple moneylending to modern banking was a natural and inevitable step. Both in India and certain South-East Asian countries their business ventures proved to be remarkably successful. Their personalised and painstaking methods of banking, their particular system of book-keeping, their law-abiding nature and their philanthropic activities resulting in substantial contributions to a variety of good causes are worthy of detailed chronological documentation and evaluation.[14]

An American observer writing about the Nagarathars in Burma points out: ' The Chettiars are Saivites, and always established a temple in every area where any number of them conducted business. The temple became the centre of the local Chettiar community and often the headquarters of business operations. In Rangoon, the temple's six "apartments" were on the ground floor, and on the second floor was a shrine of Shiva with space in front for meetings of the community to settle current rates and other matters of general importance. The mere physical arrangements of these temples with the idols and the cash boxes stored under the same roof, illust-

[14]A few distinguished Nagarathar philanthropists have apparently understood early in life Andrew Carnegie's maxim that ' surplus wealth is a sacred trust which its possessor is bound to administer to the good of the community '.

rate most vividly the complete identification of the religious and the economic.

'The first thing demanded of a Chettiar was honesty. According to the *Burma Provincial Banking Enquiry Committee Report* dishonesty was punished by complete severance from the caste; and all those whose conduct contributed to losses through dishonesty were called upon to make good the amount. This is a built-in insurance, indispensable to the successful operation of the community, for not only does a reputation of honesty enhance the Chettiar prestige with his customers, but the freedom with funds, which was allowed all agents and employees required trustworthiness.'[15]

From ancient times, a percentage of the profits of all Nagarathar firms has been set apart for charity. This custom, called *Mahimai* in Tamil, is akin to that of ancient Jews and certain present-day Christian groups who believe in giving regularly a share of their monthly income—tithing—to the maintenance and support of the church to which they belong and the worthy causes which the church may espouse.

As this feature of *Mahimai* or tithing in India is near unique to this community it needs a little elaboration. In the old days a Nagarathar moneylending firm usually set aside a percentage of profits in the name of the deity or the idol they worshipped as a partner. This was in the nature of an irrevocable gift to the idol. Apart from a portion of the profits that are set aside for charity in the name of the deity, the food prepared everyday in the Nagarathar temple is dedicated to the idol, and after the *puja* (worship ceremony) is over, distributed to the devotees and the poor.[16]

[15]Allene Masters, 'The Chettiars in Burma: An Economic Survey', *Population Review* (Madras), Vol. 1, No. 1, January 1957.

[16]This worthy custom of giving a part of one's earnings to charity, or the particular way this custom was carried out among the Nagarthars overseas, has not been without legal complications, at least in Malaya (now Malaysia).

In Attorney-General v Thirporee Sondree (Thirupurasundari) Justice Ford (1874–1 Ky 377) (apparently moved by an iconoclastic zeal) held that a gift of money to an Idol for the benefit of a temple is void as being an absurdity and not a charity, but that was long before the true nature and status of an Idol in the context of Hindu religion was appreciated in Malaya. The Idol is a legal entity known to the law and has a juridical status with the power of suing and being sued and his shebait is the manager of his estate. This was forcibly pointed

In the past and until the nineteen-twenties, the Nagarathar philanthropy, apart from helping the needy members of the community, was largely directed to the renovation of ancient Hindu temples in India, particularly in Tamil Nadu and South India, the construction of new Saivite temples in several cities overseas where the community established itself and its business operations, the donation of landed property, the revenue of which was used in perpetuity to defray the expenses involved in maintenance of the temple, its priests and the observance of rituals of daily worship and periodical religious festivals, and the building and maintenance of choultries (religious inns) where visiting Hindu pilgrims were housed and taken care of.

But in recent decades, both before and after the advent of India's freedom, Nagarathar philanthropy has been directed to schools, colleges and universities as well as clinics and hospitals, in keeping with the altered attitudes and changed concepts of social weal and public welfare.

Similarly the occupational composition of the Nagarathar population has significantly changed. Today the community while still preeminently involved in banking and trading, is diversi-, fied and reflects the normal occupational composition of any present-day Indian or Asian population group.

Apart from such conventional professions as medicine, engineering, law and teaching, the community is involved in a wide spectrum of business and commercial operations including the manufacture of a variety of modern industrial goods, textile mills, cement and rayon factories, construction operations, export and import businesses.

out by Lord Shaw in the Privy Council in *Pramitha Nath Mullick v. Pradyumna Kumar Mullick* (1925–52 IA 245). His Lordship observed, ' One of the questions emerging at this point, is as to the nature of such an idol, and the services due thereto. A Hindu Idol is, according to long established authority, founded upon the religious customs of the Hindus, and the recognition thereof by Courts of Law, a juristic entity. It has a juridical status with the power of suing and being sued. Its interests are attended to by the person who has the deity in his charge and who is in law its manager with all the powers which would, in such circumstances, on analogy, be given to the manager of the estate of an infant heir. See S. K. D., ' Nattukkottai Chettiars in Malaya ', *The Malayan Law Journal*, February 1958.

The community on the whole has made good its business and cultural heritage in becoming a relatively affluent group in the nation's economy, and its philanthropic contribution to the State and the people in general (and not just to the Nagarathar community alone) is considerably larger than its population numbers would warrant. If a careful accounting is rendered of all their benefactions, large and small, in India and elsewhere over the last century, the total may well run into many millions of rupees. In this, they are not unlike the Parsees, the Marwaris, and the American and European Jews, noted through the centuries for their small numbers and large benefactions.

# IV

# NAGARATHARS IN LEGEND AND HISTORY

## 1. Sources of Data

The history of the genesis, growth and dispersal of the Nagarathar community is lost in the mists of legendary antiquity.

Normally, the general sources for the history of any community or region in India can be roughly grouped under the following headings: (1) literary sources (written accounts by the natives, visitors and travellers, in terms of books, manuscripts, diaries, letters, etc.; (2) inscriptions in temples, monuments or other public places and other epigraphic material; (3) numismatic evidence; (4) grants and deeds (given by princes, rulers or community leaders for the distinguished performance of various duties by prominent citizens, expressed in palm leaf notations or copper plate announcements); and other categories.

There are, however, no reliable historical sources to provide material for even a brief authentic history of the Nagarathar community, except for two slender sources of an epigraphical nature often cited by writers on this subject: the *Velangudi* inscription and the *Pattayams* (palm leaf manuscripts) of Palani temple.

## 2. The Velangudi Inscription

The Velangudi inscription refers to a twelfth-century Tamil inscription in a Saivite temple in the Velangudi village, Tirupattur taluk of Ramanathapuram district. This inscription is generally known as Poonkonrai Velankudi; it is also sometimes referred to as Kundakkādu Velankudi. While earlier writers on the subject of Nagarathar history have contended that this inscription is an authentic and major source of Nagarathar history, they have maintained in the same breath that there is no trace whatsoever of the actual inscription, nor a photostat or any other reliable copy of it, and that attempts to locate the actual inscription have failed.

At the end of the last century, however, a South Indian writer, Sadhavadanam Subramaniya Ayyar, about whom little is known, brought out a Tamil book entitled *Thanavaisyar ākiya Nattukottai Nagarathar Sarithram* (Thanjavur: Desabimani Press, 1894).

This book is believed to have been based on a manuscript kept in the Mutt of Tulavur (which is a small village situated near Kunnakkudi of Ramanathapuram district). This manuscript, in its turn, is alleged to be based on the Velangudi inscription.

Material in this book by Subramania Ayyar on the history and particularly the various historical migrations of the Nagarathars, supposedly based on the Velangudi inscription, has found its way into numerous subsequent Tamil publications.[17] And the various dates, periods and incidents mentioned therein have been taken seriously enough by a few modern scholars for them to dilate upon the ancient history of the community, the rise and fall of its fortunes and its periodical mass migrations from one region to another in Tamil Nadu.

The so-called history given in Ayyar's book begins from 2898 B.C. and ends in A.D. 1565. Three migrations are referred to in the book. The first two movements were from Naga Nadu to Tondaimandalam, and from Tondaimandalam to Chola Nadu. And the third and last was from Chola Nadu to Pandia Nadu.

[17]These are: Chockalinga Ayyah, *Nattukkottai Nagarathar enum Magudatana Vaisyarin Marabu Vilakkam* (Karaikudi: Periyannan Chettiar, 1919).

A. Ramanathan Chettiar, *Nattukkottai Nagarathar Varalaru* (Madras: Commercial Printing and Publishing House, 1953).

A. Seshadri Sharma, *Nattukkottai Nagarathar Varalaru* (Madras: Vanadhi Publishing House, 1970).

CT. Natarajan, *Nattukkottai Nagarathar Varalaru* (Nachandupatti: Somu, 1973)

This 'history' is full of fascinating details with dates in Salivahana[18] and Kali[19] eras.

All this was supposed to be based on the important Velangudi inscription — according to Ayyar the only major source of information on Nagarathar history available thus far. But the few South Indian historical scholars working on this minute bit of history from 1894 onwards apparently did not find the actual Velangudi inscription.

Fortunately, the present writer was able to locate the inscription and obtain a photostat copy of it, thanks to the Epigraphist of Dravidian Inscriptions of the Archaeological Survey of the Government of India, Mysore Circle. This twelfth-century Tamil inscription, and an English translation of it, are reproduced elsewhere in this book. We presume it is the true Velangudi inscription, and there seems to be no reason to doubt it. The inscription does not give any historical material on the evolution and migration of the Nagarathar community at all. It simply mentions the gifts given by the Vanipa Nagarathars of Velangudi to the God of the temple at Velangudi, and nothing more!

Therefore, all that has been written on the Nagarathar history based on this spurious source during the last nearly a century, must be taken merely as a community legend. In a word, to the knowledge of the present writer, there is no acceptable, reliable evidence on which to construct even a skeletal scholarly history of the community.

## TRANSLATION OF THE INSCRIPTION No. 507 OF 1958–59 FROM VELANGUDI (D) TIRUPPATTUR TALUK, RAMANATHAPURAM DISTRICT

Hail! prosperity! In the fifth year opposite the first year of *Sadaiyavarman* alias *Tribhuvana Chakkaravarthikal Vikrama Pandya Dēvar,*[20] we, the *Vāṇiya Nagarathar*[21] of Vēlaṅguḍi in *Poonkuṇra*

[18]Salivahana Era commences from A.D. 78.

[19]Kali or Kaliyuga era is reckoned as beginning from 3102 B.C.

[20]Sadaiyavarman Vikrama Pandya was a ruler of Pandya country (Southern Tamil Nadu)—thirteenth century.

[21]Nagarathars of Merchant Community.

*Nādu,*[22] have assigned to the God (Nāyanār) the following taxes: We caused the aforesaid rights to be incised on the temple wall. They are as follows: *Pāḍi Kāval*[23] tax levied on the people (Ūrār) — two old *Kāsus*[24] per year, tax on pepper —. . kāsus per one bundle (Pothi), two and half kāsus per one bundle of arecanuts, two and half kāsus per a bundle of sesame, one and one by eighth kāsus per a bundle of paddy, two and half kāsus per a bundle of rice, two and half kāsus per one bundle of cotton and one and one by eighth kasus per a bundle of salt; Thus agreed the officers and the Ūrār of Vēlaṅguḍi. Further we, the *Vāniyar* (of Vēlaṇguḍi) agree to give one piece of oil cake (to the temple).

### 3. Pattayams

The second source usually cited is the Records of Palani Temple or the *Pattyams* of Palani. Palani is a small town near Dindugal in Madurai district. The town has a temple on a hill dedicated to the Saivite God Thandayuthapani. These *Pattayams* are palm leaf manuscript records in Tamil. Dr. V.SP. Manickam, former Professor of Tamil at Annamalai University, has edited the eight Palani *Pattayams.*[25]

The names of these eight Palani records and their approximate dates are given below:

1. *Nirampa Aalakiya Desikar Pattayam* — A.D. 1627
2. Palani Temple current table — A.D. 1670
3. Seven Nagarathar *Dharmasasanams* — A.D. 1680
4. Seven Nagarathar *Dharmasasanams* — A.D. 1766
5. Seven Nagarathar *Dharmasasanams* — A.D. 1788
6. *Pranmalai Adeenam Current Table* — A.D. 1800
7. *Adeenam Pattabisheka Table* — A.D. 1802
8. *Madalaya Dharmasasanam* — A.D. 1805

[22]Area around Mahibalanpatti, Tiruppattur taluk, Ramanathapuram district.

[23]System of watch in a village.

[24]An ancient gold coin=28 gr. troy.

[25]V. SP. Manickam (ed.), *Nagarathar Arappattayankal* (Nerkuppai: Annathana Madam, 1961).

## Velangudi Inscription

1 ஸ்வஸ்தி ஸ்ரீ [1 1*] கொச்சடையபன்மரான திரிபுவனசக்க[ர்*]வத்
வ தி

2 திகள் ஸ்ரீ விக்(கி)ரம பாண்டிய தெவர்க்கு யாண்டு ரு ஆவதோ
[மா[சி*]மு]

3 பூங்குன்ற நாட்டு வேலங்குடி வாணிய நகரத்தொம் எங்கள்
தெ-

4 ருவில் பாடிகாவல் நாயநார்க்கு குடுத்தொம் ந[க*]ரத்தொம்
சவத்தி

5 யடர் பகல் வாணிய நகரத்தொம் கல்வெட்டி
குடுத்தொம் உடர்

6 ஆண்டொன்றுக்கு இறக்கும் பழங்காசு இரண்டும்
பெரு மிளகு கெ

7 பாதிக்கு காசு .. ம் பாக்கு பொதி ஒன்றுக்கு காசு உஇம்
என் பொதி க

8 க்கு கா[சு*] உஇ ம் நெற்பொதிக்கு காசு கறும்
அரிசி பொதிக்கு காசு உஇ ம் பருத்தி பொ-

9 திக்கு காசு உஇ ம் உப்பு பொ[தி*]க்கு காசு கற ம்
இப்படிக்கு வெலங்குடி முதலி-

10 களும் ஊரும் அமைஞ்சு சொல்ல இப்படி செய்து
குடுத்தொம் இவ்வூ ர் வா-

11 ணியரொம் ??? பனைவால் ஒருகட்டி பிள்ளைக்கும்
குடுப்பொமா

12 கவும் ??? — ~

In characters of about the twelfth century.

[*] indicates letters supplied where they are not engraved.

[ ]—not clear.

. - letter not decipherable or broken.

These Palani *Pattayams* are written in colloquial Tamil. They mention the original and traditional salt business (*Uppu Vaniham*) of the Nagarathar community, their contributions to the Palani Temple and their other religious activities in connection with this temple during the seventeenth and eighteenth centuries. During this period this region was ruled by the Telugu Nayak Kings of Madurai, and the Sivaganga part of the Nayak Kingdom was under the tutelage of the Maruthu Pandya brothers who ruled the tiny Sivaganga State in Ramanathapuram district between A.D. 1780 and 1801.

There are a few noteworthy points in these records. In the second *sasana* or *sasanam* (a deed or a declaration on a palm leaf or copper plate) we come across for the first time the term *pulli* denoting a married couple (' dot ' in Tamil)[26] and *pullikasu* (money for each dot). It says that every Nagarathar *pulli* should give some amount, mutually agreed upon between the temple authorities and the Nagarathar, for the maintenance of the Palani Temple and for the regular performance of certain religious functions. In other *sasanas* also these terms are used in connection with the collection of contributions for this purpose. Here the term *pulli* is considered equivalent to *kudi* (family). From these records we come to know that the term *pulli* came into use among the Nagarathars and their temple records from about A.D. 1670

Another term, *vellatti* (wife), occurs a few times in these records. In one of the Nagarathar legends (to be narrated shortly) there is the story of Nagarathar men marrying *Vellala* girls. The Nagarathars are generally considered to belong to the traditional third caste (*Vaisyas*) of merchants and traders. And the *Vellalas* belong to a sub-group of the fourth caste of agriculturists. This is, of course, intercaste marriage. According to the evidence available in the *sasanas*, the term *Vellatti* clearly means wife.[27] The wife of

[26]Later in this essay we shall deal with the practice and importance of entering a married couple as a dot (*pulli*) in the temple records.

[27]The term *Vellatti* occurs in *Isaikudimanam*, a marriage agreement prevalent even now in the Nagarathar community; and a line in the marriage agreement says ' Vellattikku panam muppadu ' which means thirty panams (silver coins) to Vellatti.

a man named Kumarappan in the records is called *Vellatti Cittal.* The term *Acchi*, used in the present day for a Nagarathar housewife, had not yet come into vogue.[28]

In the above mentioned *sasanas* we come across for the first time in the literature available to us the somewhat peculiar way in which the traditional Nagarathars write their names. We find such names as Murugappa Chetty Veerappan and Arunachalam Chetty Ramanathan. These mean Veerappan, son of Murugappa Chetty, and Ramanathan, son of Arunachalam Chetty respectively. Even in the *moy* (customary cash presented by invitees to social functions) accounts written during the time of marriage, the names of bridegrooms are referred to as above. It is apparently not customary to say Murugappa Chetty's son (*magan*) Veerappan but simply Murugappa Chetty Veerappan. This practice continues to a large extent to this day in all agreements, legal and otherwise.

The contribution of the Nagarathar community to the growth of Tamil language and literature is attested to in one of the *sasanas.* There are references to the Nagarathar's love for poet Tiruvalluvar's (circa first century A.D.) famous book *Tirukkural* and the saint Thirumular's (circa fifth century A.D.) Saivite work *Tirumantiramālai.* The *sasanas* also bear evidence to the rich patronage extended by the Nagarathar community to Tamil poets and writers in general. For example, a golden anklet was bestowed upon *Avvai*, the celebrated Tamil poetess; the community also constructed a temple in memory of Kamban, the renowned author of the Tamil *Ramayana.*

As for legends tracing the history of the community from the earliest times, there is no dearth whatsoever. If a community's legends may be taken to reflect some kernel of historical truth (no matter how distorted and embellished) from generation to generation, we have then some rough outline of the genesis, growth, internal migration and diaspora of the community through the last two centuries.

[28]One writer, Mr. Saw Ganesan, however, believes that *Vellatti* means a maidservant. He probably finds it difficult to reconcile such intercaste marriages two centuries ago or even earlier.

Saw Ganesan, *Pillaiyarpatti Talavaralaru* (in Tamil) (Pillayarpatti: P. K. Nagaramaniyam, 1955) p. 59.

## 4. Two Tamil Epics

The major literary sources; *Silappadikaram* and *Manimegalai*, the two earliest Tamil epics, believed to have been composed in the second and sixth centuries A.D. respectively, throw some light on the Nagarathars in general and their socio-economic activities of the period in particular.

As for the epic *Silappadikaram*, it is considered important for its hero and heroine, Kovalan and Kannagi, belong to the Vaisya caste and the Nagarathar (or Nattukkottai Chettiar) sub-community. There is some internal circumstantial evidence based on the traditional mores of the community which lend a certain amount of credence to this belief.

The interesting story of *Silappadikaram* may be briefly told for the benefit of the non-Tamilian reader.

Kovalan and his wife Kannagi are a happy couple of the affluent merchant community. They live in comfort in the city of Kaveri-poom-pattinam,[29] the flourishing capital port of the Chola Kingdom in circa second century A.D.

One day Kovalan happens to meet the beautiful dancer Madhavi, and loses his heart over her charms. He becomes involved with her to the extent of almost entirely forgetting his wife Kannagi. In course of time he deserts Kannagi and leaves with Madhavi. After a few years, during the *Indra Vizha* festival celebrations he unjustly suspects Madhavi's fidelity, forsakes her, and returns to Kannagi, who has been faithfully awaiting the return of her errant husband.

After a happy reunion, both Kovalan and Kannagi come to Madurai, the then capital of the Pandya Kingdom, to start their lives afresh. Kovalan sets out to sell one of Kannagi's anklets. It so happens that at that time the Queen of the Kingdom had lost one of *her* anklets, and the servants of the court had been searching in the city for the lost royal ornament. Kovalan is caught while trying to sell his wife's anklet, and a false charge is foisted on him

[29]Kaveri-poom-pattinam (the Khaberis of Ptolemy) is now a village in Sirkali taluk of Tanjore district where the river Kaveri (Cauvery) enters the sea. In earlier Tamil literature the village is also called Poompuhar, sometimes abbreviated as Puhar.

as the thief responsible for the Queen's missing anklet. Without enquiring into the question of his innocence or guilt, the Pandyan King orders Kovalan's summary execution.

On hearing this shocking news, Kannagi rushes to the Pandyan Court and proves her husband's innocence by producing her other matching anklet. The King, shocked by the weight of his inordinate injustice, collapses and dies on the spot. So does the Queen. But the death of the royal couple does not assuage Kannagi's anguish over her husband's tragic end. With a supernatural wrath and power born of her righteousness and chastity, she casts a curse on the city of Madurai and reduces it almost to ashes. Thus the death of her innocent husband has been avenged.

And true to all Hindu epics, there is a happy ending. The Goddess of Madurai, the presiding deity of the city, appears before Kannagi and pacifies her. Kannagi, calmed and consoled, ascends the western hills where her husband awaits her in a heavenly vehicle. The wife and husband, thus miraculously reunited, depart for happy regions unknown.

Certain references to the habits and manners of Kovalan and Kannagi are reminiscent of the Nagarathars of the present day. Even certain Tamil terms used then by the poet Prince Ilango Adigal, the author of *Silappadikaram*, are apparently in current colloquial usage by the Nagarathars. Thus Kovalan and Kannagi might well have belonged to the trading community which we have now come to call the Nagarathars.

Some believe that the present-day Nagarathars are descended from the Vaisya community referred to in the *Silappadikaram*. The word ' Chetty ' appears for the first time in the epic. Certain customs like blowing a conch on all ceremonial occasions (it is, however, possible that this custom was practised earlier by certain other Hindu communities), taking the *tali* (the chain with which the bridegroom solemnises his marriage with the bride), in procession before tying it round the neck of the bride, the arrangement for a married son to have a separate establishment in the same house, etc., are also cited as evidence to prove that the Nagarathars are at least as old as the epic.

We learn from the *Manimegalai*, another Tamil epic, that a rich merchant named Chandradattan, possibly a forefather of the

Nattukkottai Chettiars, sailed from India to Malaya and other South-East Asian countries in his own sailing boat, in the period which may be reckoned roughly to have been some time during the beginning of the Christian era. The Nagarathars apparently practised the oft-quoted Tamil saying *thirai kadalōdium thiraviyam thēdu* meaning that one must acquire wealth, going even beyond the high seas to do so.

Tamil literature of the period refers to the Chettiars' flourishing trade — including overseas trade — in cotton textiles, pearls, spices and silk.

Writing about the social life of the Tamils during the Sangam period (circa fifth century A.D.), Dr Subrahmanian points out:

'It seems from a note in the *Nachchinarkiniyam*[30] that 'trade' is common to *Vaisyas* and to *Vellalas*. It appears that (1) learning, (2) performing sacrifices, (3) making gifts, (4) agriculture, (5) protection of cows and (6) trade were the prescribed duties of a *Vaisya*, while, (1) learning, other than the Vedas, (2) making gifts, (3) agriculture, (4) protection of cows, (5) trade and (6) worship are the prescribed functions of a *Vellala*. But another list says that worship must be substituted by performing sacrifices for, in as much as they enjoyed *jus connubium* with royal families, they could also perform such sacrifices as the kings performed. But it seems that considerable confusion existed between the *Vaisyas* and the *Vellalas* and they were known mostly by the profession they, for the time being, pursued. The merchants and the traders largely belonged to the cities; Puhar was a most famous place for the great *Vaisya* families to which Kannagi and Kovalan belonged. The name *Chetti* denoting a commercial community of South India seems to have been known in the *Sangam* age also. We come across a merchant called *Arattan Chetty*[31] in the *Silappadikaram*; the *Manimegalai* speaks of 'Chandradattan' a merchant as a *chetti*[32] and mentions nine other *chettis* in another context.[33] These *chettis*

[30]*Nachchinarkiniyam* is a commentary on *Tholkappiyam*, the earliest extent Tamil Grammar and the former was written by the famous commentator Nachchinarkiniyar of the fourteenth century A.D.

[31]*Silappadikaram*, XXIII: 129.

[32]*Manimegalai*, XVI: 107.

[33]*Manimegalai*, XXV: 165.

were merchants. They were the richest community in the land; among them were the richest persons in the capital city with the possible exception of the kings. The suburb of the city in which they lived was 'like the very house of the goddess of wealth.'

'The foreign trade which is known to have been very extensive in the *Sangam* age was managed by the *Vaisyas*. While the fishermen owned the small fishing boats, the big merchants owned the bigger ocean-going vessels. They lived in luxurious houses and led a high life'.[34]

Another literary source for some fragmentary information about the Nagarathars is Sekkilar's[35] *Periyapuranam*, an epic of the twelth century which narrates the biographies of some sixty-three Saivite saints who flourished in Tamil Nadu between the third and the sixth centuries. A few of these saints are Nagarathars, notably Pattinathar[36] who is believed to have flourished in Chettinad around the ninth century.

## 5. A Modern Literary Source

A more modern literary source is found in the poetical works of Pāduvār Muthappa Chettiar of Kilasivalpatti village. He lived in the earlier part of the nineteenth century and his writings, particularly the book *Thirumuga Vilasam*,[37] throw some light not

[34]N. Subrahmanian, *Sangam Polity: The Administration and Social Life of the Sangam Tamils* (Bombay: Asia Publishing House, 1966) pp. 279-280.

[35]Seikkilar was a Prime Minister of a Chola King and a famous Saivite poet, during the twelfth century.

P. Ramanathan Pillai and S. A. Ramaswamy (eds.), *Tiruththondar Maakkathai (Periyapuranam)* (Madras: The South-India Saiva Siddhanta Works Publishing Society, 1970).

[36]It is evident from the history of Tamil literature that there have been two poets of the name, Pattinathar, the first, an erudite Saivite sage of ninth or tenth century and the second a *Siddha* or mystic of seventeenth or eighteenth century. The first one wrote five poems in about 210 verses, running to about 2,000 lines, gathered into the eleventh Book of the Saiva canon. The second one also composed mostly occasional verses running about 2,000 lines which are grouped under the name *Pattinathar Padal Thirattu* (Collection of Pattinathar's Verses).

[37]Pāduvār Muthappa Chettiar, *Jayakondar Sadagamum Tirumuga Vilasamum Nattukkottai Nagarathar Sarithramum* (Madras: Saiva Siddhanta Noorppathippu Kazhagam, 1941).

only on the recent history of the community but also on their social and religious beliefs and practices.

Several legends speak of the Nagarathar community's migration *en masse* from one kingdom to another in the Tamil country until about the seventeenth century when they settled down in what is now Chettinad.

The Nagarathars' original home is believed to be either Kanchipuram or Kaveri-poom-pattinam. From Kanchipuram, as a resuit of heavy and unjust fines and punishments imposed upon them (the reasons for such unjust treatment are not clear), the Chettiars moved to the Chola country. According to one story, Manunidhi Cholan, a righteous ruler of the Chola country of the day, enquired of the Chettiars the reasons behind their sudden mass 'immigration' into his realm. On hearing of their past affluent history and their current tale of woe in Kanchipuram, the King was kind enough to permit them to settle in his kingdom. He then bestowed certain royal honours on them. He is believed to have told them, 'We regard you as *Pradhana Vaisyas* [important traders] and you will be given the rare honour of placing the crown on the head of the prince who succeeds to the throne. As such you will be called *Makuda Vaisyas* (*Makuda* means a crown).'

The King allotted them enviable residential quarters in the east, west and south streets of the capital Kaveri-poom-pattinam. Apparently the north street of the capital was reserved for ordinary Vaisyas. The Nagarathars were given a lion flag or standard and were permitted to display golden *stupi* (*kalasam* or golden vessel) on their homes and to receive religious orders from Isanya Sivachariar of Chidambaram.

Thus some eight thousand families settled in the capital. They developed a flourishing trade and served the King with unswerving loyalty. In course of time they earned even a higher title, for they came to be called *Rathina-dana-makuta Vaisyas* (meaning Vaisyas or merchants dealing in precious stones, possessing considerable wealth and acting as crown-bearers of the Chola Princes).

Such royal hospitality did not go unreciprocated. The Nagarathars were not only loyal and law-abiding citizens but became noted for their piety and philanthropy. They continued their worship of Vinayaka or Ganesha, the god that gives success, followed the path of Saivism, built temples and tanks and sank public wells.

A century or so later, an irretrievable tragedy overtook the Vaisyas. The traditional accounts of what happened vary, but the popular version is that King Poovanti Cholan made advances to a young Vaisya woman and when she refused him, he imprisoned all the Vaisya women. It is not clear whether the King had all the women he had imprisoned murdered, or whether he freed them, and the Vaisya males, on a question of honour, put an end to their women. After this incredible catastrophe the Vaisya men gave up their lives in a mass suicide. Only the young Vaisya boys escaped this mass destruction.

As the years passed and the wicked Poovanti Cholan became old, he wished to celebrate the coronation of his son, Rajabhushana Cholan. He had, however, not forgotten that according to the existing custom a chosen leader of the Vaisyas had to crown his son. The Vaisya lads, who were being brought up by a religious leader, came to the King and said, 'Oh King! Thanks to your unrighteousness all our elders gave up their lives in honour of their women. We have no parents. There are no women in our community. Are we, young unmarried men, entitled to crown your heir apparent?'

Thereupon the King consulted various elders and gurus at his Court and found that the Vaisyas could marry the young women of the Vellala community. After prolonged consultations and negotiations with the leaders of the Vellala community, it was agreed that Vellala young women would marry the Vaisya young men. But the young Vaisya men, while willing to marry Vellala girls, were emphatic that they would not give their future daughters in marriage to Vellala men. This was the old Hindu problem of the merits of *anuloma* versus *pratiloma* marriages.[38] After some

[38] *Anuloma* marriage is one in which the groom belongs to a higher caste than that of the bride. *Pratiloma* marriage is one in which the groom belongs to a lower caste than that of the bride.

The *Pratiloma* (*prati-loma* or 'counter-hair' or marriage 'against the grain') or a hypogamous marriage is regarded as contrary to the prescribed order. The *anu-loma* ('with the hair') or hypergamous marriage though not encouraged was widely practised.

protest the Vellala young men agreed to this. Under royal patronage mass marriages were performed between Vaisya men and Vellala girls. After this matrimonial alliance the Chettiar community gained new names. They came to be called *Upayakula Poopala Vaisyas*, *Rathina-dana-makuta Poopala Vaisyas*, *Chandra Gangakula Vaisyas*, etc.[39]

There was one more move, and this was the last migration of the Chettiars within the Tamil country before they finally settled down in what is now Chettinad in Tamil Nadu. This internal migration from Chola Nadu to Pandya Nadu came about this way. Soundara Pandiyan, King of the Pandya country, approached Prince Rajabhushana Cholan and said, 'My fellow King: Our country was submerged for some time due to an unprecedented deluge. As a result, my land, people and cattle suffered much. Some people perished and many emigrated. But now the country is returning to normalcy and prosperity is round the corner. Kindly give us some good citizens and Vaisya merchants to settle in our land.' Finding the plea a reasonable one, the Chola King persuaded some Vaisya merchants to migrate to the neighbouring kingdom. The Vaisyas were willing but pointed out to the King that 'there was no point in some of us being here and some of us being there. We would like to stay united wherever we are.' Thereupon the Chola King permitted them to go to Pandya Nadu *en masse*.

As promised, King Soundara Pandyan allotted the new Vaisya immigrants some well-defined territory in his land, west of the sea, north of the river Vaigai, east of the mountain Piran-malai and south of the river Vellaru. It was here that they built their first

[39]According to another version of this legend, once when the river Cauvery was in flood and threatened to overflow the capital of the Chola Kingdom, King Poovanthi Cholan, who was the ruler at the time, proclaimed that all adult citizens should help dam the river's bank and prevent flooding of the city. The members of the Nattukkottai Chettiar community, having grown proud and conceited on account of their wealth and status, slighted the royal proclamation demanding manual labour from all men and women. The King was enraged at the Chettiar's behaviour and as a result they lost his favour. In course of time, the community was subjected to endless humiliations. The King confiscated their property. Abduction of their women and massacre of the men followed. This tragedy left behind only the Chettiar children, who were taken by some kind neighbours to the nearby Pandyan Kingdom, where they were brought up.

community centre called Ilayatrakudi Nagaram and the people who settled in this central *Nagaram* or township came to be called Nagarathars. Then they built the first temple, to be followed in course of time by eight others.

The legendary history narrated so far has been briefly summarised in essentially the same form by the British Gazetteer author, Edgar Thurston more than half a century ago:

'Oppressed by a certain ruler, the Vaisyas of lunar race living in the town of Santhyapuri emigrated in a body to Kancheepuram in the Tondamandalam country in the year 204 of the *Kaliyuga*. The King of Kancheepuram gave them permission to settle in his country and made grants of lands, temples and *Madams* [religious establishments] to them. They stayed there for a very long time, but being troubled by heavy taxes and fines, they left that part of the country about 2312 *Kaliyuga* and settled in the Chola country. The Chola King being much impressed with them, bestowed on them the privilege of placing the crown on the head of a new ruler at the time of coronation. In those days, the town of Kaveri-poom-pattinam is said to have been in a flourishing state, and in it the north street was occupied by Vaisyas from other countries. Being unwilling to disturb them, the King made the new settlers occupy the east, west and south streets. As a mark of respect they were allowed to use flags with the figure of a lion on them and use golden vessels (*kalasam*) in their houses. They all at the instance of the King, became disciples of the Isanya Sivachariyar of Pathan-jalikshetra (Chidambaram).

'About 3775 *Kaliyuga* Puvanthi Chola Raja imprisoned several of the Vaisya women, whereon all the eight thousand Vaisya families destroyed themselves leaving their male children to be taken care of by a religious teacher named Admanadhachariar. In all 1,502 children were thus brought up. Later on Poovanthi Chola fell ill, and knowing his recovery to be impossible, sent for the Vaisya boys and asked them to attend to the coronation of his son, Rajabhushana Chola. But they said that as they were bache-lors they could not comply with his request. The King made them marry Vellala girls. Those of the west street took as wives girls of the Karkathar section; those of the east street, girls of Sozhia section; and those of the south street, girls of the Kaniyala section.

The three groups became disciples of three different *Madams* [religious establishments] namely, those at Tiruvarur, Kumbakonam and Vanchium [towns]. Later, a Pandya King named Sundara Pandya is said to have asked the Chola King to induce some of the Vaisyas to settle down in the Pandya territory. They accordingly once more emigrated in a body and reached the village of Onkarakudi on a Friday. They were allowed to settle in the tract of the country north of the river Vaigai, east of the Piranmalai and south of the Vellar [river].'[40]

The present area of Chettinad thus formed part of the Pandya Kingdom until the advent of the Nayak rulers of Madurai, who held sway over the territory during the sixteenth century. At the beginning of the eighteenth century, Raghunatha Sethupathi (1674–1710), the ruler of Ramnad, defeated the Nayak army of Princess Mangammal in 1702 and secured complete freedom for his little kingdom. Between the fourteenth and seventeenth centuries, there were periodical incursions by Muslim chieftains, both from the north and the south, as well as petty feuds between Ramanathapuram and Sivaganga principalities. The consequent insecurity as well as the growth of the Chettiar population led to their gradual dispersal into nearby villages and thus the ninety-six villages of the Nagarathar community came into existence .

By 1800 the British had established their rule in South India, created the Madras Presidency and restored relatively peaceful conditions. The Nagarathars then moved closer to the centre of their settlement from the relatively far-off villages, and the Nagarathar villages shrank from the original ninety-six to the present seventy-eight.

## V

## THE NAGARATHARS' NINE TEMPLES AND THE PULLI SYSTEM OF MARRIAGE (AND POPULATION) REGISTRATION

A major and distinctive socio-religious characteristic of the Nagarathar community is their life-long association with one of

[40]Edgar Thurston, *Castes and Tribes of Southern India* (Madras: Government Press, 1909), Vol. V, p. 158.

their nine ancestral temples in Chettinad. The temples play a prominent role in Nagarathar life. A popular Nagarathar saying through the centuries has been, ' Do not live in a place where there is no temple.' (*Koil illa ōōril kudi irukka vendam.*) The Nagarathars are classified or categorised on the basis of their allegiance to a particular temple circle, for every Nagarathar by birth is a member of a temple circle through patrilineal descent, and the members of each temple circle are therefore agnates. That is, all members of temple circle are descendants of a common ancestor.

## 1. The Social Ecology of the Temple

Each of the nine 'clans' or sub-divisions of the Nagarathars own one of these temples which serves as a central meeting place for matters spiritual and temporal affecting the community.

Each of these temples represents the final authority in all religious and social matters for each of the nine clans. The administration of these matters is vested in a standing committee for each temple which is elected annually. They decide such questions as are referred to them. For example, they may arbitrate the partition of an estate between the sons and daughters of a member of the estate who died intestate. Perhaps the most important task of these temple authorities is to arrange marriages between members of the different temple clans, for members of the same temple cannot marry. And members of all the nine temple groups meet annually at some central place to discuss matters of common interest.

These nine temples are Ilayathangudi, Mathur, Vairavanpatti, Nemam, Iluppakudi, Suraikudi, Velangudi, Pillaiyarpatti and Iraniyur.[41] They are located in and around the villages of Chettinad. The first three are the big temples and have seven, seven and three sub-divisions or sub-circles respectively, totalling seventeen sub-circles. The remaining six temples are single temple circles devoid of any sub-circles. Thus there are twenty-three sub-circles in all.

[41]The names of the temples are not the same as the names of the villages in which they are located except for two temples which are Ilayathangudi and Pillaiyarpatti.

who are in charge of the day-to-day management of the temple. In addition to the *Karyakaras* who act as *Panchayatdars* (familiar in India's rural self-governing institutions) each temple has an assistant called *Vairavi* and an attender called *Thandalkaran* whose primary duty is to collect a kind of tax from the members of the temple for its maintenance.

As pointed out earlier, this Council also sometimes acts as a court of justice of sorts. It discusses and settles various matters pertaining to the overall welfare of the Nagarathar community. These issues may range from marriage contracts, monetary disputes and cases of indebtedness to deviations from the accepted norms in the conduct and behaviour of the community members. The temple's Council of Elders is naturally extremely jealous of the good name of the community whether in India or abroad.

The procedure for the settlement of disputes is a simple one. Normally the aggrieved party lodges his complaint to the temple manager who sends word to the members of the committee concerned. The complainant and defendant are summoned to attend a Council meeting and the evidence is recorded by the temple manager. When final decisions are reached after weighing the evidence and hearing both sides of the dispute, they are conveyed orally and not recorded in writing. But in the case of certain major issues, once the conciliation is over and the disputants reach an agreement, their signatures are obtained to the final award of the Council. It is surprising how often the verdict is accepted by the disputants. On such occasions when the verdict is not accepted, the Council enforces its decree first by refusing to give flower garlands at the time of marriage (which means the marriage cannot be solemnised) and secondly by exercising the more severe power of ex-communication from the community. The influence of the Council of Elders in preventing needless, expensive and time-consuming litigation is noteworthy. This does not, of course, mean that in modern times there is no litigation among the Nagarathars. But its magnitude is considerably lessened because of the good offices of the Committee of Elders.

The kind of justice which is meted out by the Temple Council of Elders has an interesting history. In the olden days there were among the Nagarathars two kinds of Panchayats called *Madathu*

*Vasal Mariyal* (*Mutt* or *Madam* or religious establishment panchayat) and *Kovil Vasal Mariyal* (temple panchayat). Both these terms denote a kind of protest in front of the Mutt and the Temple respectively. Only disputes between members of the same temple could be aired here. The complaint was usually raised by the plaintiff against the defendant with a witness in front of the temple. As soon as the plaintiff has made his complaint he was expected to go into his temple and write down the protest he had made. Then the temple authorities sent this information to the defendant who was expected to go to the temple with his reply, normally before it closed for the day. The temple authorities would then appoint a Committee of Panchayatdars or judges to go into the plaint and reach a decision. Until the decision was reached the defendant would be prevented from residing or taking his meal in the common choultry of the Nagarathars of that temple.

## 2. Temples and Trade

An interesting feature of the Nagarathars' business and religious life is reflected in the way virtually all the Nagarathars conduct their commercial transactions.

Whenever a new business was started a traditional Nagarathar would enter the credits in the new account first in the names of the God and Goddess of the temple, then in his own name, and last in the name of his village.

Apart from this, the Nagarathar businessman would set aside a certain amount or share as a fund in the name of God. There would be a separate account for this fund and sometimes a separate business also would be started from it in order to augment it. The Nagarathar businessman would evince as much interest in the business conducted in the name of God as in his own personal business concern.

Besides this, as noted earlier, a Nagarathar businessman would normally set aside a fixed percentage of the profits of his commercial undertakings for charity. This is called *mahimai*. From this income demarcated for charity the Nagarathars constructed in the old days temples dedicated to God Subramania in such new areas where they settled as Colombo, Rangoon, Singapore, Kuala

Lumpur, etc. In India, these funds were usually utilised in repairing and renovating ancient Saivite temples and to underwrite the expenditure involved in certain periodical traditional festivals connected with and conducted by the Hindu temples. We have some evidence that this kind of charity to promote Hindu religious institutions was practised by the Nagarathars from at least the sixteenth century, if not earlier. As noted earlier, we have some information from the Palani temple records of a sixteenth-century Nagarathar named Kumarappan, a salt trader, who had set aside a portion of his income to the temple of Velayuthaswamy of Palani and its religious activities.

The local Nagarathar temples, apart from the nine major temples, play an important part in various village festivities. In addition to the numerous conventional responsibilities of the temples, they play a particularly unique role during weddings. The bride or bridegroom from another village will be invited first to the local temple to offer worship and only then to the house where the marriage function will take place (of tying the *thali* round the neck of the bride). These functions are called *Pennalayppu* (welcoming the bride) and *Mappilayalayppu* (welcoming the groom).

The temple halls afford a meeting place for the Nagarathars for various secular functions as well as weddings and religious discourses. The temple is used for dances, dramas, music, receptions, public lectures and general social gatherings.[43]

And last, these temples have proved to be a refuge not only to the Nagarathars but to all Indians during times of floods, famine and public disturbances. During recent anti-Indian riots in Sri Lanka and Malaysia, these temples provided not only shelter and food but safety from the violence of the local dominant ethnic groups. Thus the Nagarathar temples have played and continue to play a tremendous role in the economic, social and religious life of the Indian minorities abroad.

[43]The present writer has enjoyed the hospitality of the Nagarathars in their temples where he has addressed Nagarathar audiences in at least half a dozen countries overseas in South-East Asia.

### 3. The Pulli System

Every Nagarathar temple in Chettinad maintains a register of all the Nagarathar marriages in the community under a system of classification called *pullis*. *A pulli* literally means a dot in Tamil.

A marriage between two Nagarathars can be solemnised only after receiving wedding garlands from the respective temples to which the families of the bride and groom belong. When a couple get married their marriage is recorded in a special Register (book) kept for the purpose in the temple (*Koil* or *Kovil*) in Tamil and with the recording of the wedding the couple become a full *pulli* in the record of the temple to which the bridegroom belongs.

The married couple (*pulli*) forms the social unit of the community, and each such unit has to contribute financially *pulli-vari* (dot-wise) and *asti-vari* (property-wise) for the maintenance of the temple.

In brief, only when a person becomes a *pulli* is he or she recognised as a bonafide member of the Nagarathar community. And what enables one to become a *pulli* is wedlock, registered in a temple to which the bridegroom's party belongs. Thus the *pulli* system is a temple-based registration of all Nagarathar marriages.

This is a remarkable institution, for among the millions of Hindus through the ages there has never been any official—governmental or religious—registration of the Hindu weddings on the lines of the Western system or in the way that the Christian and Muslim marriages are registered in India. The Hindu marriage has been purely a religious ceremony and the Hindu priest had no official status comparable to the Christian or Muslim priests in this matter.[44] It is commendable to note that the Nagarathars, who constitute such a tiny section of the Hindu population, are the only community in India, to the knowledge of the present writer, to have originated this fascinating practice of their temples keeping a record of all weddings of their members.

[44]In fact, the present writer has been pleading with the Government of India, both within Parliament and outside, for the compulsory registration of all the Hindu marriages, for legal, statistical and a variety of other purposes. But this plea has so far (1978) been in vain.

On the subject of compulsory registration o the Hindu marriages, see S. Chandrasekhar, *Population and Law in India*, 2nd ed. (Madras: Macmillan, 1978), pp. 56-59.

A husband and wife with unmarried children will retain their *pulli*. The entire family is represented by the full *pulli* of the parents. The children on their marriage will become separate individual *pullis*. It may be noted that while a marriage between two Nagarathars gives rise to a new *pulli*, a marriage between a Nagarathar and a member of any non-Nagarathar caste group will not be taken into account and neither the groom nor the bride can become a *pulli*. This device is obviously to discourage inter-caste or inter-sub-caste marriages in the community.

There are two classifications of *pullis*, called *full-pulli* and *half-pulli*. The following come under the classification of *full-pulli*:

(i) Husband and wife with unmarried children.
(ii) Husband and wife without children.
(iii) Widower with or without children.
(iv) Widow with children.
(v) Children without parents.

Classification of *half-pulli*:

(i) Widow without children.
(ii) Widow with married sons and daughters.

The following illustrations may clarify the above classifications:

(i) Husband and wife with unmarried children constitute a *full-pulli*.
(ii) Husband and wife without issue also form a *full-pulli*. As parents have a right to adopt a child from their own temple circle who by wedlock may beget children and assure the continuance of the family tree, they retain *full-pulli* status.
(iii) A widower with or without children is treated as *full-pulli*, for there is a possibility for a widower to marry again. As he is already a recognised *pulli*, he will not be considered a new *pulli* and from this new alliance he may create new *pullis* through his children.
(iv) A widow with children is also considered a full-pulli so long as all her children get married. She is treated as a *half-pulli*

only after the marriage of all her children, since by that time, she cannot remarry and her *pulli* cannot create any more new *pullis.*

(v) Unmarried children (irrespective of sex) without parent will represent the *pulli* of their parents, as there is a possibility of the children forming new *pullis* by their eventual marriages. They retain the *pulli* of their parents before marriage. The *pulli* of the parents ceases to exist once all the children get married and the parents themselves pass away.

## Half-Pulli

(i) and (ii) A widow without children and a widow with married sons and daughters are considered as *half-pulli*, since widows normally do not remarry and there is no possibility to create a new *pulli.*

Thus the above classification of a *pulli* is based on the possibility of creating a new *pulli* by that *pulli.* A *pulli* is treated as *full-pulli* as long as there is a possibility for that *pulli* to give rise to any new *pulli.*

A *pulli* is treated as *half-pulli* if there is no possibility for that *pulli* to give rise to any new *pulli.*

A *pulli* ceases to exist when the couple who formed that *pulli* are dead and there is no possibility of their *pulli* to give rise to any new *pulli.*

But the *pulli* system has certain limitations. It does not help us to obtain the precise total population of the community, as there is no way of calculating the number of children a *pulli* may have. But it does help us to reckon the trend of growth or decline and the overall demographic strength of the community in terms of families. On the basis of the average size of a family one can arrive at a rough total of the Nagarathar community's population.

# BIBLIOGRAPHY

The bibliographic materials in this book relating to the Nagarathar community (Nattukottai Chettiars), available in the English language in various libraries in India, Burma, Ceylon, Indonesia, Malaysia and Singapore are presented here. These items include books, monographs, pamphlets and articles in Indian and foreign journals, reports of various governmental commissions and non-official committees, law reports, dissertations, theses and papers and speeches by prominent Nagarathars on various occasions.

Some journals in the Tamil language which deal with Nagarathars include occasionally articles in English, but these have not been included in this bibliography as readers of this book will normally have no access to such Tamil periodicals.

These source materials have been classified and cross-classified under seventeen sections. While the first ten sections pertain to the Nagarathars and their economic, social and religious activities in India and abroad, the remaining sections are primarily concerned with their activities in Burma, Ceylon, Indonesia, Malaysia, Singapore, Vietnam and other areas. The section labelled ' General ' consists of all the miscellaneous items not included in other classifications.

A companion volume to this book will shortly be published in Tamil. Its title will be நகரத்தார் ஆய்வுத்துணை நூற்தொகுதி (*Nagarathar Aivu thunai Nootrokuthi*). In this volume, a Tamil translation of the present writer's Introductory Essay on Nagarathars will be found along with an extensive bibliography on Nagarathars available only in the Tamil language. It is hoped that this companion volume will be found useful to all those who read primarily Tamil books.

## 1. GENERAL


1. Aiyangar, S. Krishnaswamy, *Some Contributions of South India to Indian Culture* (Calcutta: University of Calcutta, 1942).
2. Aiyer, P.V. Ramachandra, *Chettinad: A Narrative of a Tour of Chettinad made by Baron Pentland of Lyth, Governor of Madras in September* 1916 (London: British Museum, 1916)
3. *Annual Report of the Nattukkottai Nagarathars' Association, Madras for the year 1936* (Madras: The Progressive Printers, 1936)
4. Archer, W.G. (ed.), *The Kama Sutra of Vatsyayana* (London: George Allen and Unwin, 1965)
5. Ayyar, K.R. Venkatarama (ed.), *A Manual of Pudukkottai State* (Pudukkottai: Sri Brihadamba State Press, 1938) Vol. 1
6. ———(ed.), *A Manual of Pudukkottai State* (Pudukkottai: Sri Brihadamba State Press, 1940) Vol. II. Part I
7. ———(ed.), *A Manual of Pudukkottai State* (Pudukkottai: Sri Brihadamba State Press, 1940) Vol. II. Part II
8. Balbour, Surgeon General Edward, *The Encyclopaedia of Asia and of Eastern and Southern Asia* (London: Bernard Quaritch, 1885) Vol. II
9. Baliga, B.S. (ed.), *Madras District Gazetteers - Madurai* (Madras: Government of Madras, 1960)
10. ———(ed.), *Madras District Gazetteers - South Arcot* (Madras: Government of Madras, 1962)
11. ———(ed.), *Madras District Gazetteers - Coimbatore* (Madras: Government of Madras, 1966)
12. Barbosa, Duarte, *An Account of the Countries bordering on the Indian Ocean and their Inhabitants* (London: The Hakluyt Society, 1918)
13. Barrett, William, *Irrational Man: A Study in Existentialist Philosophy* (New York: Doubleday, 1958)
14. Bearce George D. *British Attitudes Towards India* (London: Oxford University Press, 1961)
15. Benedict. Burson, *Indians in a Plural Society: Report on Mauritius* (London: HMSO, 1961)

16. Blunt, Sir Edward, *The I.C.S.* (London: Faber and Faber, 1937)

17. Boag, G.T. *The Madras Presidency 1881-1931* (Madras: The Superintendent, Government Press, 1933)

18. Brown, D.M. *The White Umbrella: Indian Political Thought from Manu to Gandhi* (Berkeley: University of California Press, 1953)

19. Chander, R, 'Early Indian Seamen' in Silver Jubilee Committee (ed.), *The Sir Asutosh Mookerjee Silver Jubilee* Vol. III (Calcutta: University of Calcutta, 1927)

20. Chandrasekhar, S., 'The Nagarathars: The Land, The People and Their Marrige (and population) Registration System' *Population Review* (Annamalai Nagar) Vol. 20. Nos. 1 and 2. January-December 1976

21. ———, 'The Nagarathars or the Chettiars' *The Sunday Statesman* (New Delhi) 30 October 1977

22. Chettiar, Rajah Sir Muthiah, 'Presidential Address' delivered at the Federation of Indian Chamber of Commerce *The Indian Annual Register* (Calcutta) Vol. I. No. 27. January-June 1944

23. Coedés, Genge, *Les etats Hindouises et d'Indonesie* (Paris: E. de Boccard, 1948)

24. Craddock, Sir Reginald, *The Dilemma in India* (London: Constable and Co., 1929)

25. Crawfurd, John, *Journal of an Embassy from the Governor General of India to the court of Ava in the year* 1827 (London: Henry Colburn, 1834) Second edition

26. Cumpston, I.M. *Indian Overseas in British Territories:* 1834–1854 (London: Pall Mall, 1953)

27. Danielou, Alain, *Shilappadikaram The Ankle Bracelet by Prince Ilango Adigal*, Translated (London: George Allen and Unwin, 1967)

28. Delvert, Jean, *Le Paysan Cambodgien* (The Hague: Mouton and Co., 1961)

29. Dikshitar, V.R.R. *The Silappadikaram* Translated (Madras: Oxford University Press, 1939)

30. Doctor, Geetha, 'Nattukkottai Chettiars' *The Illustrated Weekly of India* (Bombay) 20 July 1975

31. Fielding-Hall, Harold, *The Soul of a People* (London: Macmillan, 1898)
32. ———, *A People at School* (London: Macmillan, 1906)
33. *Fifth Tour of H.E. The Lord Pentland: Souvenir of Madras, Madura and Ramnad Vol. I* (Madras: The Superintendent, Government Press, 1914)
34. Francis, W., *Madras District Gazetteers - Madura* (Madras: Government of Madras, 1906)
35. ———, *Madras District Gazetteers - South Arcot* (Madras: Government of Madras, 1906)
36. Furnivall, J.S., *Colonial Policy and Practice* (Cambridge: University Press, 1948)
37. Gangulee, N., *Indians in the Empire Overseas* (London: New India Publishing Company, 1947)
38. *Government of India Act, October* 1935 Cmd. 5181 (London: His Majesty's Stationery Office, 1936)
39. Gupta, Sisir, *India and Regional Integration in Asia* (New York: Asia Publishing House, 1964)
40. Hall, D.G.E. (ed.), *The Dalhousie-Phayre Correspondence, 1852-56* (London: Oxford University Press, 1932)
41. Hardgrave, Robert L., *The Nadars of Tamilland* (London: Oxford University Press, 1969)
42. Harrison, Selig S., *India - the Most Dangerous Decades* (Madras: Oxford University Press, 1960)
43. Hemingway, F.R. *Madras District Gazetteers - Trichinopoly* (Madras: Government of Madras, 1907)
44. *The Indian Emigration Act* XXI *of* 1883 *as modified upto* 5*th March* 1897 *and Rules and Notifications issued under its provisions* (*Calcutta*, 1898)
45. An Indian Journalist, " Indian Affairs - The Chettiars Deputation to England ' *The Indian Review* (Madras) Vol. XXXVI. No. 6. June 1935
46. Information Department, *Know your District - Ramanathapuram* (Madras: Government of Madras 1950)
47. Kannathal, VE., ' A Study of Typical Nagarathar Village: K. Chokkanathapuram ' Dissertation submitted in partial fulfilment of the requirements for the Degree of Master

of Arts in Economics of the Annamalai University, Annamalainagar, 1972 (unpublished)
48. Kassim, Ismail, 'The Chettiars' *New Nation* (Singapore) 24 November 1975
49. Knorr, Klaus E., *British Colonial Theories 1570-1850* (Toronto: University of Toronto Press, 1944)
50. Kodikara, S.U. *Indo-Ceylon Relations Since Independence* (Colombo: Ceylon Institute of World Affairs, 1965)
51. Kondapi, C. *Indians Overseas 1838-1949* (Bombay: Oxford University Press, 1951)
52. Krishnamurthi, S., *et al* (eds.), *Annamalai University Magazine Silver Jubilee Number* (Annamalai Nagar: Annamalai University, 1955)
53. Lamb, Helen B., *Studies on India and Vietnam* (New York: Monthly Review Press, 1976)
54. Lee-Warner, Sir William, *Life of the Marquis of Dalhousie* (London: Macmillan, 1904)
55. Macmillan, Allister, *Seaports of India and Ceylon* (London: W.H. and L. Collingridge, 1928)
56. *Manual of the Administration of the Madras Presidency* (Madras Government Press, 1885)
57. *Memorandum on the Census on British India of 1871-72* (London: Eyre and Spottiswoode, 1875)
58. *The Memorandum and Articles of the Nattukkottai Nagarathars' Association, Madras* (Madras: The Progressive Printers, 1917)
59. Moore, Lewis, *Manual of the Trichinopoly District* (Madras: Government of Madras, 1878)
60. Multum in Parvo - Notes, 'A Call to War Effort' *The Indian Review* (Madras) Vol. XLI. No. 9. September 1940
61. Nehru, Jawaharlal, *The Discovery of India* (New York: John Day, 1944, Calcutta: Signet Press, 1946)
62. Nicolson, D.G., *Correspondence Regarding the Removal of Mr. Donald Grant Nicolson from His Appointment as First Assistant Commissioner, Tenasserim and Martaban Provinces* (London: Printed for the Author, 1862)
63. A note on 'Chronicle of Events - Chief Events' *The Indian Annual Register* (Calcutta) Vol. 1, No. 14. January-June 1931

64. A note on 'The Council of State - Legislation for First Offenders' *The Indian Annual Register* (Calcutta) Vol. 1. No. 14. January - June 1931
65. A note on 'The Madras Legislative Council' *The Indian Annual Register* (Calcutta) Vol. 1. No. 14. January-June 1931
66. A Note on 'The Hammond Committee Report - On the Delimitation of Constituencies - Commerce' *The Indian Annual Register* (Calcutta) Vol. 1. No. 19. January-June 1936
67. A Note on 'proceedings of the Assembly - The Bande-Mataram Controversy: Debt Relief Bill' *The Indian Annual Register* (Calcutta) Vol. 1. No. 21. January-June 1938
68. A Note on 'The Justice Party Confernce-Proceedings and Resolutions-Reforms in Cochin' *The Indian Annual Register* (Calcutta) Vol. II. No. 21. July-December 1938
69. A Note on 'The Madras Legislative Assembly - Muslim Leaguer's Walk Out' *The Indian Annual Register* (Calcutta) Vol. II. No. 22. July-December 1939
70. A Note on 'Chronicle of Events-April 1940' *The Indian Annual Register* (Calcutta) Vol. 1. No. 23. January-June 1940
71. A Note on 'Film World - The Mahatma on the Screen' *The Indaian Review* (Madras) Vol. XLI. No.4. April 1940
72. A Note on 'Film World - Shakthi Film, Salem' *The Indian Review* (Madras) Vol. XLI. No. 11. November 1940
73. A Note on 'A High School Jubilee' *The Indian Review* (Madras) Vol. 42. No. 10. October 1941
74. A Note on 'India in Home Polity - Causes of Anti-Indian Feelings' *The Indian Annual Register* (Calcutta) Vol. 1. No. 28. January-June 1945
75. O'Malley, L.S.S., *The Indian Civil Service 1601-1930* (London: John Murray, 1931)
76. *Parliamentary Debates of the house of Commons* 5th Series, Vol.97 (London: His Majesty's Stationery Office, 1917)
77. Patterson, G., *A Geography of India, Physical, Political and Commercial* (London: The Christian Literature Society for India, 1909)

78. Perumal, Nilkan, *Glimpses of Chettimarnad* (Madras: R.J Ram and Co., 1937)

79. ———, *Chettinad* (Coimbatore: The Popu'ar Hindusthan, 1955)

80. Pillai, T.M.N., *et al* (eds.) *Annamalai University Silver Jubilee Volume 1929-54* (Annamalai Nagar: Annamalai University, 1955)

81. Pillai, K.K., *South India and Ceylon* (Madras: University of Madras, 1963)

82. Public Relations Officer, Annamalai University (ed.) *The Annamalai University Silver Jubilee Record* (Annamalai Nagar: Annamalai University, 1955)

83. *Pudukkottai State Inscription* (Pudukkottai: Pudukkottai Durbar, 1941)

84. Ragahvaiyangar, S. Srinivasa, *Memorandum on the Progress of the Mauras Presidency During the Last Forty Years of British Administration* (Madras: Government Press, 1893)

85. Rajalakshmi, K., ' Some Aspects of Nattukottai Chettiar Community ' Dissertation Submitted for the Degree of Master of Philosophy, Department ofIndian History, University of Madras, 1978. Unpublished

86. Rajan, P. T. (ed.), *Justice Party Golden Jubliee Souvenir* (Madras: Shanmugam Press, 1968)

87. Rajkumar, M. V., *Indians Outside India—A General Survey* (New Delhi: The Foreign Department of the Indian National Congress, 1951)

88. Ramanujachari, R., L. P. K. R. Ramanathan Chettiar, *et al.* (eds.), *The Annamalai University Silver Jubliee Souvenir* (Annamalai Nagar: Annamalai University, 1955)

89. Ramaswami, A., *Gazatteer of India—Salem* (Madras: Government of Madras, 1967)

90. ———, *Tamil Nadu District Gazetteer: Ramanathapuram* (Madras Government of Tamil Nadu, 1972)

91. Rao, Raja Rama, *Ramnad Manual* (Madras: Government Press, 1889)

92. *Report on the Census of British India* 1881—*General Reports* Vol. 1. (London, 1883)

93. *Report of the Indian Statutory Commission* Cmd. 3568 (London: His Majesty's Stationary Office, 1930), 17 Vols.
94. *Report of the Sanskrit Commission* (New Delhi: Government of India, 1958)
95. *Revision of Electoral Registers* 1940, *Interim Report by the Legal Secretary with Particular Reference to First Registration of Indians under the Domicile Qualification* (Robert, H. Drayton) sessional Paper III (Colombo, 1940)
96. *Revision of Electoral Registers* 1940, *Final Report by the Legal Secretary* (Robert, H. Drayton) Sessional Paper VII Colombo, 1941)
97. Richards, F. G., *Madras District Gazetteers—Salem* (Madras: Government of Madras, 1918)
98. Rose, Saul, *Socialism in Southern Asia* (London: Oxford University Press, 1959)
99. Sastri, K. R. R., *Encyclopaedia of the Madras Presidency and the Adjacent States* (Madras: Oriental Encyclopaedia Publishing Co., 1921)
100. Secretary of Ramakrishna Mission (ed.), *The Cultural Heritage of India* Vol. IV (Calcutta: Swami Nityasvarupananda, 1956)
101. *Sessional Papers of the House of Commons* Vol. VII Cmd. 9109 (London: His Majesty's Stationary Office 1918)
102. Sitaramaya, P., *History of the Indian National Congress* Vols. I and II (Madras: Congress Committee, 1935)
103. Slater, Gilbert, *Southern India* (London: George Allen and Unwin, 1936)
104. Somasundaram, J. M., ' Annamalai University Celebrates Silver Jubilee ' *Madras Information* (Madras) April 1945
105. ———, *The University's Environs* (Annamalai Nagar: Annamalai University, 1963)
106. Somervell, D. C., *English Thought in the Nineteenth Century* (London: Methuen, 1929)
107. Spate, O. H. K., *India and Pakistan* (London: Methuen, 1954).
108. Stamp, L., *A New Geography of India, Burma and Ceylon* (Bombay: Longmans, 1939)
109. *Statement Exhibiting the Moral and Material Progress and Condition of India During the year* 1930-31 House of Commons 116.

No. 66 (London: His Majesty's Stationery Office, 1932)

110. Sundaram, Lanka, *India in World Politics*, (Delhi: Sultan Chand and Co., 1944)
111. Symes, Michael, *An Account of an Embassy to the Kingdom of Ava in* 1795 (London: W. Bulmer, 1800)
112. Tinker, Hugh, *The Foundations of Local Self-Government in India, Pakistan and Burma* (London: The Athlone Press, 1954)
113. *Separate and Unequal: India and the Indians in the British Common Mealth*, 1920-1950 (London: Hurst, 1976)
114. US Department of State, *Foreign Service Dispatch No.* 2539 Unclassified, New Delhi, 19 May 1953
115. Venkataraman, V. K., *India and Her Neighbours* (Bombay: Vora, 1947)
116. Venkataswami, T., *A Manual of the Tanjore District* (Madras: Government Press, 1883)
117. Waiz, S. A. (ed.), *Indians Abroad—Directory* (Bombay,: Imperial Indian Citizenship Association, 1934).
118. Wint, Guy, *The British in Asia* (London: Faber and Faber, 1954)
119. Woodruff, Philip, *The Men Who Ruled India: The Guardians* Vol. II (London: Jonathan Cape, 1954)

## 2. LAND

120. Chandrasekhar, S., 'The Nagarathars: The Land, The People and Their Marriage (and Population) Registration System' See 20
121. Cressey, C. B., *Asia's Land and Peoples* (New York: McGraw Hill, 1951)
122. East, W. G. and O. H. K. Spate, *The Changing Map of Asia* (London: Methuen, 1950)
123. Isaac, P. M., 'Burma Government's land Purchase Schemes' *Modern Review* (Calcutta) Vol. 66. December 1939.
124. Kelly, R. Talbot, *Burma—The Land and the People* (Boston and Tokyo: J. B. Millet and Co, 1910)
125. Ooi Jin-Bee, *Land, People and Economy in Malaya* (London: Longmans, 1969)
126. Perumal, Nilkan, *Glimpses of Chettimarnad* See. 87.
127. ———, Chettinad See 79.
128. Powell, B. H. Baden, *A Short Account of the Land Revenue and its Administration in the British India* (Oxford: Clarendon Press, 1913)
129. Sastri, K. A. Nilakanta, 'The Tamil Land and the Eastern Colonies' *Journal of Greater India Society* (Calcutta) Vol. XI. 1944

## 3. POPULATION

130. Blunt, Sir Edward, 'The Environment and Distribution of the Indian People' in Sir Edward Blunt (ed.), *Social Service in India* (London: His Majesty's Stationery Office, 1938)
131. Caldwell, J. C., 'Malaysia's Population Problem' in S. Chandrasekhar (ed.), *Asia's Population Problems* (London: George Allen and Unwin, 1967) (Westwood, Conn.: Greenwood Press, 1977), second edition.
132. ———, 'New and Old Malaya: Aspects of Demographic Change in a High Growth Rate, Multiracial Society' *Population Review* (Madras) Vol. VIII. No. 2. July 1964.
133. Census of Burma (Incomplete) 1941, *Figures of Population* (Rangoon: Government Press, 1941)
134. Census of India 1871, Madras, *Statement of Population of 1871 in each Village of the Trichinopoloy District* (Madras: Government Press, 1974)
135. Census of India 1871, Madras Presidency, *Supplementary Tables of the Census Results* Vol II. (Madras: Government Press, 1874)
136. Census of India 1871, Madras Presidency, *Report* (Madras: Government Press, 1974)
137. Census of India, 1881 Madras, *Report* Vol. I (London: Her Majesty's Stationery Office, 1883)
138. Census of India 1891, Madras, *Report* Voll XIII (Madras: (Madras Government Press, 1893)
139. Census of India 1891, India, *General Report* (London: Eyre and Spottiswoode, 1893)
140. Census of India 1891, Madras, *Tables A to E British Territory, Tables for Feudatory States and a Caste Index* Vol. XV (Madras: The Superintendent, Government Press, 1893)
141. Census of India 1901, Madras *Report* Part I. Vol. XV (Madras: Government Press, 1902)
142. Census of India 1901, India *Tables* Part II. Vol. I (A) (Calcutta: Government of India, 1903)
143. Census of India 1911, Madras *Report* Part I. Vol. XII (Madras: Government Press, 1912)

144. Census of India 1911, Madras *Imperial and Provincial Tables* Part II. Vol. XII (Madras: Government of India, 1912)
145. Census of India 1921, Madras *Report Part* I. Vol. XIII (Madras: Government Press, 1922)
146. Census of India 1921, Madras *Imperial and Provincial Tables* Part II. Vol. XII (Madras Government Press, 1922)
147. Census of India 1921, Madras *Imperial and Provincial Tables* Part II. Vol. XIII (Madras: Superintendent, Government Press, 1922)
148. Census of India 1921, *Report* Part I, Vol. I (Calcutta: Superintendent, Government Printing, 1924)
149. Census of India 1931, Madras *Report* Part I Vol. XIV Calcutta: Government of India, 1932)
150. Census of India 1941, Madras Presidency *Village Statistics—Madura District* (Madras: Government Press, 1943)
151. Census of India 1941, Madras Presidency *Village Statistics—Ramnad District* (Madras: Government Press, 1943)
152. Census of India 1941, Madras Presidency *Village Statistics—Trichinopoloy District* (Madras: Government Press, 1943)
153. Census of India 1951, Madras and Coorg *Report* Part I. Vol. III. (Madras: Government Press, 1953)
154. Census of India 1961, *Madras General Population Tables* Part II-A Vol. IX (Madras: Government of India, 1963)
155. Census of India 1961, Madras *District Census Hand Book—Coimbatore* Part X-I Vol. IX. (Madras: Government of India, 1964)
156. Census of India 1961, Madras *District Census Hand Book—Tiruchirapalli* Vol. I Part X-II Vol. IX. (Madras: Government of India, 1965)
157. Census of India 1961, Madras *District Census Hand Book—South Arcot* Vol. I Part X-XII Vol. IX. (Madras: Government of India, 1965)
158. Census of India 1961, Madras *District Census Hand Book—Ramanathapuram* Vol. I Part X-VI Vol. IX (Madras: Government of India, 1965)
159. Census of India 1961, Madras *District Census Hand Book—Ramanathapuram* Vol. II. Part X-VII Vol. X (Madras: Government of India, 1965)

160. Census of India 1961, Madras *General Report* Part I-A(i) Vol. IX (Madras: Government of India, 1966)

161. Chander, Ramesh, 'Malaysia: A population Dossier' Paper Presented at the Seminar on Population Problems held for the Representatives of the Mass Media, Frasers Hill, 14-16 June1974. (Bangkok: UNESCO Regional Office for Education in Asia, 1974)

162. Chander, R. and J. M. N. (eds.), *The Population of Malaysia* Research Paper No. 102 (Kuala Lumpur: Department of Statistics 1976)

163. Chandrasekhar, S., *India's Population: Fact and Policy* (Chidambaram: Indian Institute for Population Studies, 1950) second edition

164. ———, 'The Nagarathars: The Land, The People and Their Marriage (and Population) Registration System' See 20.

165. Cressey, C. B., *Asia's Land and Peoples* See 121

166. Davis, Kingsley, *The Population of India and Pakistan* (Princeton: Princeton University Press, 1961)

167. Dey, Mukul K., 'The Ethnic Groups of Malaya: A Population Study' *Population Review* (Madras), Vol. VI No. 2, July 1962

168. Fernandez, Dorothy Z., 'Population Levels, Trends and Planning in Malaysia' Paper presented at the Third Malaysian Economic Convention, August 21-24, 1976, Penang, Kuala Lumpur: Malaysian Economic Association 1974

169. Hirschman, Charles, *Estimates of the Inter-Censal Population by Sex, Community and Age Group, Peninsular Malaysia: 1957-1970* Research Paper No 9 (Kuala Lumpur: Department of Statistics, 1970)

170. ———, 'A Note on Past and Future Trends in Population Growth in Malaysia' Unpublished Paper, Kuala Lumpur 1974

171. Jackson, James C., 'Population changes in Selangor State, 1850-1891 *The Journal of Tropical Geography* (Singapore) Vol. 19, 1964

172. Lee, Yong Leng, 'Population changes in Sabah, 1951-60' *The Journal of Tropical Geography* (Singapore) Vol. 26 June 1968

173 Lim, Chong-Yah, *Population: In Economic Development of Modern Malaya* (Kula Lumpur: Oxford University Press, 1967)

174. McGee, Terence Garry, 'Population: A Preliminary Analysis' in Wang Gunguru (ed.), *Malaysia: A Survey* (London: Pall Mall Press, 1965)

175. Pountney, A. M., *The Census of the Federated Malay States, 1911* (London: Darling, 1911)

176. Pryor, Robin J., *Bibliography on Internal Migration in South East Asia* (Canberra: Department of Demography, Australian National University, 1977)

177. Sandhu, Kernial Singh, 'Indian Migration and Population Change in Malaya, c. 100-1957 A.D.: A Historical Geography' Thesis Submitted for the Degree of Master of Arts University of British Columbia, Vancouver, B.C. 1961

178. ———, 'Some Preliminary Observations of the Origins and Characteristics of Indian Migration to Malaya, 1786-1957' in K. G. Tregonning (ed.), *Papers on Malaysian History* (Singapore: Journal South-East Asian History, 1962)

179. Saw Swee Hock and Pearl Chu, 'The Population of Nineteenth Century Penang' Paper No. 56 of the International Conference on Asian History, 5-10 August 1968, Kuala Lumpur, Department of History, University of Malaya, 1968

180. Schechtman, Joseph P., *Population Transfers in Asia* (New York: Hailsby Press, 1949)

181. Shantakumar, G., 'A note on projection of populations of national and sub-national areas in Malaya' Paper presented at the ECAFE working Group on Projections of Population on Sub National Areas, 14-23 May 1969, Bangkok, Thailand, ECAFE, 1969

182. Smith, T. E., *Population Growth in Malaya* (London: Royal Institute of International Affairs, 1952)

183. *Some Implications of Rapid Population Growth in Peninsular Malaysia* (Kuala Lumpur; The Federation of Family Planning Associations, 1973)

184. Stuart, J., ' Why Burma is Sparsely Peopled ' *Journal of the Burma Research Society* ' (Rangoon) Vol. IV. April 1914.

185. Thomson, P. A., ' The impact of culture on birth rate and population increase in the Federation of Malaya ' Paper presented at the Seventh Conference of the International Planned Parenthood Federation, 10-16 February 1963, Singapore, *Excerpta Medica, Amsterdam:* 1964

186. Turner, L. J. B., *Population tn Ceylon, Its History, People, Commerce, Industries and Reseources* (Colombo: Plate Ltd., 1924)

187. Vlieland, C. A., *British Malaya: A Report on the 1931 Census and on Certain Problems of Vital Statistics* (London: Crown Agents for the Colonies, 1932)

188. ———, 'The Population of the Malay Peninsula' *Geographical Review* (New York) Vol. 24. January 1934.

189. ———, 'The 1947 Census of Malaya' *Pacific Affairs* (New York Vol. 22, No. 1 March 1949)

190. You Poh Seng, ' The Population of Malaya ' in Lim Tay Boh (ed.), *Problems of the Malayan Economy* (Singapore: Donald Moor for Eastern Universities Press, 1965)

## 4. HISTORY

191. Abidin, B. A. D. Wahid Zainal (ed.), *Glimpses of Malaysian History* (Kuala Lumpur, Dewan Bahasa Dan Pustaka, 1970)

192. Aiyar, S. Radhakrishnan, *General History of Pudukkottai State* (Pudukkottai: Pudukkottai Durbar, 1916)

193. Aiyar, K. V. Subrahmanya, ' Seven Vatteluttu Inscriptions from the Kongu Country ' in N. Lakshminarayan Rao and D. C. Sircar (eds.), *Epigraphia Indica and Record of Archaeological Survey of India* Vol. XXX (Delhi: Government of India, 1958)

194. Antony, F. Aserappa, *A Short History of the Ceylon Chetty Community and Various Facts of General Interest* (Colombo: Catholic Press, 1940)

195. Appadorai, A., *Economic History of South India* (Madras: University of Madras, 1936)

196. Baker, C. J., and D. A. Wash Book, *South India: Political Institution and Political Change 1880–1940* (New York: Macmillan, 1975)

197. Brown, R. Grant, ' The Origin of the Burmese ' *Journal of the Burma Research Society* (Rangoon) 11 June 1912

198. Cady, John F., *Southeast Asia; Its Historical Development* (New York: McGraw Hill, 1964)

199. Caldwell, Robert, *History of Tirunelveli* (Madras: E. Keys at the Government, 1881)

200. Capper, John, *Old Ceylon or Sketches of Ceylon Life in the Olden Times* (Colombo: Ceylon Times Press, 1877)

201. Chakkravarthi, Nalini Ranjan, *The Indian Minority in Burma: The Rise and Decline of an Immigrant Community* (London: Oxford University Press, 1971)

202. Codrington, H. W., *Short History of Ceylon*, (London: Macmillan, 1929)

203. Danielou, Alain, *Shilappadikaram* See 27

204. Devahuti, D., *India and Ancient Malaya from the Earliest Times to Circa, A.D. 1400* (Singapore: Eastern Universities Press, 1965)

205. Dikshitar, V. R. R., *The Silappadikaram* See 29

206. ———, 'Setti in Literature and Epigraphy' in B. V. N. Naidu (ed.), *Rajah Sir Annamalai Chettair Commemoration Volume* (Annamalai Nagar: Annamalai University, 1941)
207. The Director of Information and Public Relatians, *Poom puhar: Art Gallery* (Madras: Government of Tamil Nadu, 1975)
208. Dodwell, H. H. and R. R., Sethi, (eds ), *Cambridge History of India* (Delhi: Chand and Co., 1958)
209. Fleet, J. F., 'Inscription at Mangoli' in E. Hultzsch, (ed.), *Epigraphia Indica and Record of Archaeological Survey of India,* Vol. V. (Calcutta: Government of India, 1959)
210. Hall, D. G. E., *A History of South-East Asia* (New York; St. Martin's Press, 1955)
211. Harrison, B., *South-East Asia: A Short History* (London: Macmillan, 1954)
212. Harvey, G. E., *History of Burma* (London: Longmans, 1925)
213. ———, 'Burma, 1782-1852' in H. H. Dodwell (ed.), *The Cambridge History of India* (Cambridge: The University Press, 1929) (This volume is the same as Vol. IV of *The Cambridge History of the British Empire*)
214. Lionel, D. Barneth, 'Tumbagi Inscription of the Reign of Satyasraya: Saka 926' in H. Krishna Sastri, (ed.), *Epigraphia Indica and Record of Archaeological Survey of India* Vol. XVII (Calcutta: Government of India, 1924)
215. ———, 'Inscriptions of Sudi' in F. W. Thomas (ed.), *Epigraphia Indica and Record of Archaeological Survey of India* Vol. XV (Calcutta: Government of India, 1925)
216. Maurice, Collis, *The Burmese Scene—Political—Historical—Pictorial* (London and New York: John Crowther, 1944)
217. Moreland, William H., and Sir Atul Chatterjee, *A Short History of India* (London: Longmans, 1955)
218. Nagarajan, K. *Chidambaram: A Chronicle Play* (Madras: The Associated Printers, 1955)
219. Netto, George, *Indians in Malaya: Historical Facts and Figures* (Singapore: The Author, 1961)
220. Paranavitana, S., 'The Polonnaruva Inscription of Vijatabahu I' H. Krishna Sastri and Herananda Sastri (eds.),

*Epigraphia Indica and Record of Archaeological Survey of India* (Calcutta: Government of India, 1925-1926) Vol. XVIII

221. Pearn, B. R. *A History of Rangoon* (Rangoon: American Baptist Mission Press, 1939)
222. Phayre, Arthur P., *History of Burma* (London: Tubner and Co., 1883)
223. Pillai, K. K. *Social History of the Tamils* (Madras: University of Madras, 1974)
224. Playne, Somerset, *Southern India: Its History, People, Commerce, and Industrial Resources* (London: The Foreign and Colonial Compiling and Publishing Co., 1915)
225. Ragavan, M. D. *The Tamils in Ceylon: India in Ceylonese History, Society and Culture* (Bombay: Allied Publishing House, 1969)
226. Ryan, N. J., *A History of Malaysia and Singapore* (Kuala Lumpur Oxford University Press, 1976)
227. Sastri, K. A. Nilakanta, *The Pandyan Kingdom* (London: Luzac and Co., 1929)
228. ———, *Studies in Chola History and Administration* (Madras: University of Madras, 1932)
229. ———, *The Cholas* (Madras: University of Madras, 1935)
230. ———, *A History of South India* Vol. 1 (London: Oxford University Press, 1955)
231. Scott, J. G., *Burma: From the Earliest Times to the Present Day* (London: T. Fisher Unwin, 1924)
232. Subramaniyan, N., *History of Tamil Nadu* (Madurai: Madurai Koodal Publishers, 1972)
233. Surianarayanan, P., History of Local Government in Ramanathapuram District with Special Reference to Municipal Government and its Relations with the District Administration and the State. Unpublished M.Litt. Thesis, Annamalai University, Annamalai Nagar, 1963
234. Tambipillai, V. J, 'The Origin of the Tamil Velalas' *Journal of the Royal Asiatic Society—Ceylon Branch* (Colombo) Vol. XXI. No. 61. 1908
235. Thiruvenkatachari, S., *The Sethupathis of Ramnad* (Karaikudi Extension Department, Dr. Alagappa Chettiar Training College, 1959)

236. Tinker, Hugh, *South Asia: A Short History* (New York: Praeger, 1966)

237. Trager, Frank N., *Burma from Kingdom to Republic* (New York: Frederick A. Praeger, 1966)

238. Tregonning, K. G. (ed.) *Papers on Malayan History* (Singapore Journal of South-East Asian History 1962)

239. Turner, L. J. B. *Population in Ceylon: Its History, People, Commerce, Industries and Resources* See 186

240. Verhoeven, F. R. J, 'Some Notes on the History of the Tamil Country in Dutch Malacca (1641-1825)' in Xavier S. Thaninayagam (ed.), *Proceedings of the First International Conference—Seminar of Tamil Studies* Vol. 1 (Kuala Lumpur: International Association of Tamil Research, 1969)

241. Wickremasinghe, D. M. De (ed.), *Epigraphia Zeylanica Being Lithic and other Inscriptions of Ceylon* Vol. II. (London: Government of Ceylon by Humphrey Milford, 1928)

242. Winstedt, R. O., *The Malaysian Cultural History* (London: Routledge and K. Paul, 1961)

## 5. SOCIETY

243. Aiyar, P. R. Sundara, 'Concerning the Nattukkottai Chettiars *Malabar Quarterly Review* (Cochin) 1905

244. Ampalavanar, Rajeswary, 'Social and Political Developments in the Indian Community of Malaya, 1920-41' Thesis Submitted for the Degree of Master of Arts, University of Malaya, Kuala Lumpur, 1969. Unpublished

245. Angangco, Ofelia Regale, 'The Indian Community in the Philippines' M.A. Thesis, University of Philippines, Manila, 1956. Unpublished

246. Antony F. Aserappa, *A Short History of the Ceylon Chetty Community and various Facts of General Interest* See 194

247. Arasaratnam, S., 'Social and Political Ferment in the Malayan Indian Community 1945-1955' in Xavier S. Thaninayagam (ed.) *Proceedings of the First International Conference—Seminar on Tamil Studies* Vol. 1 (Kuala Lumpur: International Association of Tamil Research, 1969)

248. Ariyapala, M.B. *Society in Medieval Ceylon* (Colombo: De Silva 1956)

249. Bailey, F.G., *Caste and Economic Frontier* (Manchester: University Press, 1957)

250. ———, *Tribe, Caste and the Nation* (Manchester: University Press, 1960)

251. Bhattacharya, J. N., *Hindu Castes and Sects* (Calcutta: Thacker, 1896)

252. Census of India 1961, Madras *Food Habits in Madras State* Part XI-B Vol. IX (Madras: Government of India, 1964)

253. Census of India 1961, Madras *Family Planning Attitude in Madras City* Part XI-F Vol. IX (Madras: Government of India, 1966)

254. Chandrasekhar, S., 'The Nagarathars: The Land, The People and Their Marriage (and Population) Registration System' See 20

255. ———, 'The Nagarathars or the Chettiars' See 21

256. Chetty, Simon Casie, *Caste, Customs and Manners and Literature of the Tamils* (Colombo: Ceylon Printers, 1934)

257. Cole, Fay-Cooper, *The Peoples of Malaysia* (Princeton: D. Van Nostrand, 1945)

258. Geary, Grattan, *Burma after the Conquest, Viewed in Its Political Social and Commercial Aspects from Mandalay* (London: Marston, Searle and Rivington, 1886)

259. Ghurye, G. S. *Caste and Class in India* (Bombay: The Popular Book Depot, 1950)

260. Hagen, E.H. *On the Theory of Social Change* (Homewood, Illinois: The Dorsey Press, 1962)

261. Hardgrave, Robert L., *The Nadars of Tamilnadu—The Political Culture of a Community in change* (Berkeley: University of California Press, 1969)

262. Hughes, David R., *The Peoples of Malaya* (Singapore: Donald Moore for Eastern Universities Press, 1965)

263. Hutton, J.H., *Caste in India: Its Nature, Function and Origin* (London: Oxford University Press, 1963)

264. Jumabhoy, R., *Multiracial Singapore* (Singapore: Mubaruk, 1970)

265. Kaur, Amarjit, 'North Indians: A Study of their Economic, Social and Political Activities with Special Reference to Selangor, 1870s-1940s' Thesis Submitted for the Degree of Master of Arts, University of Malaya, Kuala Lumpur, 1973. Unpublished

266. Mahadevan, Raman, ' Pattern of Enterprise of Immigrant Enterpreneurs - A Study of Chettiars in Malaya ' *Economic and Political Weekly* (Bombay) Vol. XIII. No. 4. January 1978

267. ———, ' Pattern of Enterprise of Immigrant Entepreneru s— A Study of Chettiars in Malaya ' *Economic and Political Weekly* (Bombay) Vol. XIII. No. 5. February 1978

268. Mani, A., ' Caste Among Singapore Hindus ' *Commentary* (Singapore) Quarterly Journal of the University of Singapore, November 1975

269. McTaggart, W. Donald, ' The Distribution of Ethnic Groups in Malaya, 1947-57' *The Journal of Tropical Geography* (Singapore) Vol. 26. June 1968

270. McTaggart, W. Donald and Duane Stormont, *Mapping Ethnic Groups in Malaysia* (Tempe, Arizona: Center for Asian Studies, Arizona State University, 1974)

271. *Memorandum submitted by Nagarathar Federation, Madras to the Backward Classes Commission Government of Tamil Nadu* Madras, 1971

272. Mootheden, A. Varkey, *Our Countrymen in Malaya: Being a Review of the Social, Economic and Political Position of Indians in Malaya* (Trivandrum: V. V. Press, 1932)

273. Nadarajah, Devapoopathy, *Women in Tamil Society* (Kuala Lumpur: University of Malaya, 1969)

274. Nadarajan, M., ' The Nattukkottai Chettiar Community and South-East Asia ' in Xavier S. Thaninayagam (ed.), *Proceedings of the First International Conference—Seminar of Tamil Studies* Vol. 1 (Kuala Lumpur: International Association of Tamil Research, 1966)

275. Netto, George, *Indians in Malaya: Historical Facts and Figures* (Singapore: The author, 1961)

276. Pillai, K.K., *Social History of the Tamils* See 223

277. Planning Forum, *Socio-Economic Survey of Pallathur, Ramanathapuram District* (Pallathur: Seethalakshmi Achi College for Women, 1968)

278. ———, *Socio-Economic Survey on Impact of Higher Education on the views and Marriage Practices Among the Teaching Staff and Student Community in the Seethalakshmi Achi College* (Pallathur: Sri Seethalakshmi Achi College for Women, 1969)

279. Rabeendran, R., *Ethno-racial Marginality in West Malaysia: The Case of the Peranakan Hindu Melaka or Malacca Chitty Community* (Kuala Lumpur: Department of Anthropology and Sociology, University of Malaya, 1976)

280. Ragavan, M.D., *The Tamils in Ceylon: India in Ceylonese History, Society and Culture* See 225

281. Schwartz, Barton M. (ed.), *Caste in Overseas Indian Communities* (San Francisco: Chandler Publishing Co., 1967)

282. Sherring, M.A., *Hindu Tribes and Castes* 3 Vols. (Calcutta: Thacker, 1881)

283. Singaravelu, S., *Social Life of the Tamils* (Kuala Lumpur: Department of Indian Studies, University of Malaya, 1966)

284. Singer, Milton, *Krishna: Myth, Rites and Attitudes* (Chicago: University of Chicago Press, 1968)

285. ———, *When a Great Tradition Modernizes: An Anthropological Approach to Indian Civilization* (New York: Praeger, 1972)

286. Subramaniyan, N., *The Sangam Polity: Administration and Social Life of Tamils* (Bombay: Asia Publishing House 1966)

287. Sundaram, Lanka, *Indians Overseas: A Study of Economic Sociology* (Madras: G. A. Natesan, 1933)

288. Thurston, Edgar, *Castes and Tribes of Southern India* Vol. V. (Delhi: Cosmo Publications, 1975)

289. Turner, L. J. B. *Population in Ceylon, Its History People Commerce, Industries and Resources* See 186

290. Wiebe, Paul D. and S. Mariappan, 'Ethnic Insularity and National Identification in a plural Society: Indian Malaysians: A Case Study' *Economic and Political Weekly* (Bombay) 13 September 1975

## 6. ECONOMIC ACTIVITIES

291. Adas, Michael, *The Burma Delta: Economic Development and Social Change on an Asian Rice Frontier 1812-1941* (Madison: University of Wisconsin Press, 1974)

292. ———, 'Immigrant Asians and the Economic Impact of European Imperialism: The Role of the South Indian Chettiars in British Burma' *Journal of Asian Studies* (Durham) Vol. 33. No. 3. 1974

293. Ady, Peter, 'Economic Bases of Unrest in Burma' *Foreign Affairs* (New York) No. 3. April 1951

294. Aiyer, V. G. Ramakrishna, *The Economy of a South Indian Temple* (Annamalai Nagar: Annamalai University, 1946)

295. Alavi, Hamza, 'India and the Colonial Mode of Production' *Socialist Register* (London) 1975

296. Allen, G. C. and Audrey G. Donnithorne, *Western Enterprise in Indonesia and Malaysia: A Study in Economic Development* (London: George Allen and Unwin, 1962)

297. Andrew, E. J. L., *Indian Labour in Rangoon* (London: Oxford University Press, 1933)

298. Andrus, J. R. *Rural Reconstruction in Burma* (London: Oxford University Press, 1936)

299. ———, 'Three Economic Systems Clash in Burma' *The Review of Economic Studies* (London) February 1936

300. ———, 'Foreign Investments in Burma' *Pacific Affairs* (New York) Vol. XVII. March 1944

301. ———, 'The Agrarian Problem in Burma' *Pacific Affairs* (New York) Vol. XIX. No. 3. September 1946

302. ———, *Burmese Economic Life* (Stanford: Standford University Press, 1947)

303. Annamalai, R., 'The Role of Nattukkottai Chettiar Community in the Economic Development of Sri Lanka' Paper presented to the Indian Congress at its 30th Session Bhuvaneshwar, 1977

304. *Annual Season and Crop Reports of Burma* 1929-40 (Rangoon: Government Press, 1929-40)

305. Anstey, V., *The Economic Development of India* (London: Longmans Green and Co., 1929)

306. Appadorai, A., *Economic Conditions of South India 1000-1500* 2 Volumes (Madras: The University of Madras, 1936)
307. ———, *Economic History of South India* See 195
308. Arasaratnam, S., 'Aspects of the Role and Activities of South Indian Merchants, C. 1650-1750' in Xavier S. Thaninayagam (ed.) *Proceedings of the First International Conference—Seminar of Tamil Studies* Vol. 1. (Kuala Lumpur: International Association of Tamil Research, 1966)
309. Bailey, F. G., *Caste and Economic Frontier* See 249
310. *Banking Enquiry Committee's Report* 1930 (Rangoon: Government Press, 1930)
311. Baster, A. S. J., *The Imperial Bans* (London: P. S. King, 1929).
312. Bennholdt - Thomsen, Veronika, 'Probleme der Klassenanalyse des Agrarsektors in Staaten Weltmarktabhangiger Reproduction' Working Paper, Programme in Development Studies, University of Bielefeld, 1977
313. Bennison, J. J., *Report of an Enquiry into the standard of Living of the Working Classes in Rangoon* (Rangoon: Superintendent Government Printing, 1928)
314. Berna, James J., (S.J.) Entrepreneurship in Madras State, India' Unpublished doctoral dissertation, Columbia University, New York City, 1958
315. Binns, B. O., *Agricultural Economy in Burma* (Rangoon: Superintendent, Government Printing, 1948)
316. Callis, Helmut G., *Foreign Capital in South-East Asia* (New York Institute of Pacific Relations, 1942)
317. *Census of Professional and Institutional Establishments, Private Sector* (Kuala Lumpur: Department of Statistics, 1977)
318. *Ceylon Banking Commission Report* Vol. I. Ceylon Sessional Paper XXII (Colombo, 1934)
319. *Ceylon Banking Commission Report - Evidence of Indian Mercantile Chamber of Ceylon* Vol. II. (Colombo, 1934)
320. Challis, Joyce, *Annotated Bibliography of Economic and Social Material: West Malaysia* Part I (Singapore: Economic Research Centre, University of Singapore, 1968)

321. ———, *Annotated Bibliography of Economic and Social Material in Sabah and Sarawak* Part I (Singapore: Economic Research Centre, University of Singapore, 1969)

322. ———, *Annotated Bibliography of Economic and Social Material in Singapore and West Malaysia* (Singapore: Eeonomic Research Centre, University of Singapore, 1969)

323. Chattopadhyaya, Haraprasad, 'Nattukkottai Chettiars in the Economy of Sri Lanka *The Calcutta Historical Journal* (Calcutta) Vol. 1. No. 2. January-June 1977

324. Cheah Boon kheng, 'Money Lenders' *The Strait Times* (Kuala Lumpur) 23 October 1972

325. Chettiar, M. C. T. M. Chidambaram, 'The Southern India Chamber of Commerce' in Madras Tercentenary Committee (ed.), *Madras Tercentenary Commemoration Volume* (Madras: Madras Tercentenary Committee, 1939)

326. Chettiar, Rajah Sir Muthiah, *Presidential Address to the Fderation of Chambers of Commerce and Industry* (New Delhi: FCCI 1943)

327. Christian, John Leroy, *Modern Burma: A Survey of Political and Economic Development* (Berkeley: University of California Press, 1942)

328. Clayton, H., *Rural Development in Burma* (Rangoon: Superintendent, Government Printing, 1911)

329. Codrington, H. W., *Ceylon Coins and Currency* (Colombo: Memoirs of the Colombo Museum, Luzac, 1924)

330. Colaco, Lucy, 'Labour Emigration from India to the British Colonies of Ceylon, Malaya, and Fiji during the Years 1850-1921 Dissertation Submitted for the Degree of Master of Arts, University of London, London, 1957

331. Cooper, Chester L. 'Money-lenders and the Economic Development of Lower Burma: An Exploratory Historical Study of the Role of Indian Chettiars' Unpublished Ph.D. Dissertation, American University, Washington, D.C. 1959

332. Darling, Malcolm L., *The Punjab Peasant in Prosperity and Debt* (London: Oxford University Press, 1925)

333. ———, *Note on the Cooperative Movement in Burma* (Rangoon: Superintendent, Government Printing, 1937)

334. Das, A. B. and M. N. Chatterji, *The Indian Economy, Its Growth and Problems* (Calcutta: Bookland, 1957)
335. Day, D.H., 'The Nattukkottai Chettiars of Tamil Nadu: Explorations in the Economic History of an Entrepreneuri al Community' *South Asian Varia* (Syracuse: Syracuse University, 1972)
336. *Divisional Reports on the Working of the Indian Factories Act in Lower Burma, 1898-1911* (Rangoon: Superintendent, Government Printing, 1899-1912)
337. Diwanjee, C. H. 'Bills Market in South India' *The Indian Review* (Madras) Vol. 38. No. 7. July 1937
338. Donnison, F. S. V. *Public Administration in Burma: A Study of Development During the British Connexion* (London: Royal Institute of International Affairs, 1953)
339. D.C. (Probably Duroiselle Charles) 'A Handbook of Indian Companies Act' *Journal of the Burma Research Society* (Rangoon) Vol. II. 1912
340. Economic Planning Board, Government of Burma. *Two-Year Plan* (Rangoon: Superintendent, Government Printing, 1948)
341. Evers, Hans-Dieter, 'Chettiar Moneylenders in South East Asia' Paper presented at the VI European Conference on Modern South Asian Studies, Paris July 8-13, 1978 (Mimeographed)
342. Federated Malay States, *Report and Proceedings of the Committee to Consider Why the System of Small Loans to Native Agriculturists had failed in Perak* Perak 1912
343. *First Annual Report on the Progress Made Giving Effect to those Recommendations of the Royal Commission of Agriculture in India, 1928 Which Concern Burma* (Rangoon: Superintendent-Government Printing, 1929)
344. Firth, Raymond, *Malay Fisherman: Their Peasant Economy* (London: Routledge and Kegan Paul, 1966)
345. *Fiscal and Economic Annual of Burma* (Rangoon: Bureau of State Printing Presses, 1943)
346. Fonseka, H. N. C., 'Agricultural Colonisation of the Dry Zone by the Ceylon Tamils' in R. E. Asher (ed.), *Proceedings of the Second International Conference-Seminar of Tamil*

*Studies* Vol. 2. (Madras: International Association of Tamil Research, 1971)

347. Furnivall, J. S., *An Introduction to the Political Economy of Burma* (Rangoon: Burma Book Club 1938)
348. Geary, Grattan, *Burma After the Conquest, Viewed in Its Political, Social and Commercial Aspects from Mandalay* See 258
349. Geertz, Clifford, *Agricultural Involution* (Berkeley: University of California Press, 1968)
350. Government of Burma, *A Handbook of Agriculture for Burma* (Rangoon: Superintendent, Government Printing, 1898)
351. ———, *Agriculture in Burma* A Collection of papers written by the Government for the Royal Commission on Agriculture, 1926–28 (Rangoon: Superintendent, Government Printing, 1927)
352. ———, *Agricultural Leaflets* (Rangoon: Superintendent, Government Printing, 1927)
353. ———, *The Marketing Crops in Burma* (Rangoon: Superintendent, Government Printing, 1928)
354. ———, *List of Industrial Establishments in Burma* 1929 (Rangoon: Superintendent, Government Printing, 1929)
355. ———, *List of Industrial Establishments in Burma*, 1933 (Rangoon: Superintendent, Government Printing, 1933)
356. ———, *List of Industrial Establishment in Burma*, 1936 (Rangoon: Superintendent, Government Printing, 1936)
357. ———, *Trade in Agricultural Products* (Rangoon: Superintendent, Government Printing, 1939)
358. ———, *Economic Survey of Burma* Published annually (Rangoon: Superintendent, Government Printing, 1951–1958)
359. Grant, J. W., *The Rice Crop in Burma: Its History, Cultivation, Marketing and Improvement* (Rangoon: Superintendent, Government Printing, 1949)
360. Gubbay, M. M. S., 'Indigenous Indian Banking' *Journal of the Royal Society of Arts* (London) 2 December 1927
361. ———, *Indigenous Indian Banking* (Bombay: D.B. Taraporevala, 1928)
362. Gunasekara, H. A. de. S., *From Dependent Currency to Central Banking in Ceylon* (London: The London School of Economics and Political Science, 1961)

363. Hagen, Everitt Einer, *The Economic Development of Burma* (Washington: National Planning Association, 1956)

364. Hawley A. H., Z. Dorothy, Fernandes and Vasantha Kandiah *The Expectation of Working Life in Peninsular Malaysia, 1970* Research Paper No. 8 (Kuala Lumpur: Department of Statistics, 1974)

365. Henrickson, S., ' The Indian Business Communities and the Evolution of an Industrialist Class ' (Calcutta: Chamber of Commerce, 1955.) Mimeographed Paper

366. Huke, Robert E., ' Rice in Burma: A Geographic Analysis of Three Agricultural Villages ' Unpublished Ph.D Dissertation, Syracuse University, Syracuse 1953

367. *Indian Overseas Bank: Survey of Ramanathapuram District* (Madras, 1971)

368. Indrapala, K., ' Some Medieval Mercantile Communities of South India and Ceylon ' *Journal of Tamil Studies* (Madras) 1970

369. Institute for Techno-Economic Studies, Madras. *Project Report of Ramnad District* (Madras: Government of Tamil Nadu, 1973)

370. *Interim Report of the Committee Appointed to Enquire into the Rice and Paddy Trade* (Rangoon: Superintendent, Government Printing, 1935)

371. Ito, Shoji, ' Inde ne Chushe Zaibatsu ne Sesei to Genjo-Chetia no Baai ' (The Rise, Development and present condition of the smaller financial groups in India. Chettiars and others) Part I and II, in *Ajia keizai* (Tokyo) Vol. 5. Nos. 11-12 November-December 1964

372. ———, ' A Note on the Business Combine in India, with Special Reference to the Nattukkottai Chettiars ' *The Developing Economies* (Tokyo) Vol. A. 1966

373. Jackson, R. N., *Immigrant Labour and the Development of Malaya, 1786-1920* (Kuala Lumpur: Government Press, 1961)

374. Jacoby, E. H., *Agrarian Unrest in South-East Asia* (Bombay: Asia Publishing House, 1961)

375. Jagatheesan, N. ' Immigration of Indian Labour into Malaya, 1867-1910 ' Thesis Submitted for the Degree of Bachelor of Arts, University of Singapore, Singapore, 1954

376. Jain, J.P., *Indian Banking Analysed* (Delhi and Madras: Banking Experts, 1953)

377. Jain, L.C., *Indigenous Banking in India* (London: Macmillan, 1929)

378. ———, *The Monetary Problems of India* (London: Macmillan, 1933)

379. Jain, Ravindra K., *Migrants, Proletarians or Malayan?—South Indians on the Plantation Frontier in Malaya* (Canberra: Australian National University, 1965)

380. *Ramanathapuram Experiment: Paradigm of An Estate-farm-factory Community in Malaya* (Armidale, New South Wales: Faculty of Agricultural Economics, University of New England, 1966

381. Jain, R. K., *South Indians on the plantation Frontier in Malaya* (Kuala Lumpur: University of Malaya Press, 1970)

382. Karunatilake, H. N. S., *Banking and Financial Institutions in Ceylon* (Colombo: Central Bank of Ceylon, 1968)

383. Kasper, Wolfgang, *Malaysia: A Study in Successful Economic Development* (Washington: American Enterprise Institute for Public Policy Research, 1974).

384. Kaur, Amarjit, 'North Indians: A Study of their Economic, Social and Political Activities with Special Reference to Selangor, 1870s-1940s'. See 265.

385. Knappen, Tippetts, Abett Mccarthy, *Comprehensive Report: Economic and Engineering Development Prepared for the Government of the Union of Burma* 2 Volumes (Alyesbury, England, 1953)

386. Knowles, L. C. A., *The Industrial and Commercial Revolutions in Great Britain During the Nineteenth Century* (London: George Routledge and Sons, 1926).

387. Krishnan, V., *The Indigenous Banking in South India* (Bombay: Bombay State Co-operative Union, 1959)

388. Krishnaswami, S. Y., *Rural Problems in Madras* (Madras: Government Press, 1947).

389. *Labour Policy in General including the Enforcement of Labour Measures: Preparatory Asiatic Regional Conference of the Inter-National Labour Organisation* Report II (New Delhi: International Labour Office, 1947)

390. Leach, F. Burton, 'The Rice Industry of Burma' *Journal of the Burma Research Society* (Rangoon) Vol. XXVIII. April 1937

391. Lim Chong-Yeh, *Population: In Economic Development of Modern Malaya* See 173

392. Lim, David, *Economic Growth and Development in West Malaysia 1947-1970* (Kuala Lumpur: Oxford University Press, 1973).

393. Lim, Tech Ghee, *Peasants and their Agricultural Economy in Colonial Malaya 1874-1941* (Kuala Lumpur: Oxford University Press, 1977)

394. *The Lower Burma Land Revenue Manual* (*Containing the Lower Burma Land and Revenue Act of* 1876) (Rangoon: Superintendent, Government Printing, 1938)

395. Ma, Ronald and Yon Poh Seng, 'The Economic Characteristics of the Population of the Federation of Malaya, 1957. *Malayan Economic Review* (Kuala Lumpur) Vol. 5. No. 2 October 1960

396. Mackenzie, Sir Compton, *Realms of Silver: One Hunderd Years of Banking in the East* (London: Routledge and Kegan Paul, 1954)

397. Mahadevan, Raman, *The Origin and Growth of Enterpreneurship in the Nattukkottai Chettiar Community of Tamil Nadu 1880-1930*. M. Phil. Thesis (New Delhi: Jawaharlal Nehru University, 1973)

398. ———, 'Pattern of Enterprises of Immigrant Enterpreneurs—A study of Chettiars in Malaya' See 266.

399. ———, 'Pattern of Enterprise of Immigrant Entrepreneurs—A Study of Chettiars in Malaya' See 267.

400. Mahalingam, T. V., *Economic Life in Vijayanagar Empire* (Madras: University of Madras, 1951)

401. Marjoribanks, N. E., and A. K. G. Ahmad Tambi Marakkayar, *Report on Indian Labour Emigrating to Ceylon and Malaya* (Madras: Government Press, 1971)

402. Masters, Allene, 'The Chettiars in Burma: An Economic Survey of a Migrant Community' *Population Review* (Madras) Vol. 1. January 1957

403. Mayer, Adrian, C., 'Aspects of Credit and Debt among Fiji Indian Farmers' *Journal of the Polynesian Society* (Wellington, New Zealand) Vol. 64. 1955

404. McEachern, 'The Mode of Production in India' *Journal of Contemporary History* (London) Vol. 6. No. 4. 1975

405. *Memorandum of Financial Settlement between Burma and India* (London: His Majesty's Stationery Office, 1931)

406. Mills, L. A., *Malaya*: A *Political and Economic Appraisal* (Minneapolis: University of Minnesota Press, 1958)

407. *Mobilization of Domestic Capital in Certain Countries of Asia and the Far East* (Bangkok; Economic Commission for Asia and the Far East 1951)

408. Mookerji, Radhakumud, *Indian Shipping* (London: Longmans, 1912)

409. ———, 'Indian and Chinese Labour in the Agriculture of South-East Asia' *Modern Review* (Calcutta) Vol. LIV. No. 6. 1933

410. Mootheden, A., Varkey, *Our Countrymen in Malaya: Being a Review of the Social, Economic and Political Position of Indians* in Malaya See 272.

411. Morris, A. P., *Report on the Development of Industries in Burma* (Rangoon: Superintendent, Government Printing, 1920)

412. Multum in Parvo—Notes 'Currency and Banking—Imperial Bank Governors' *The Indian Review* (Madras) Vol. 35 No. 2. February 1934

413. Muranjan, S. K., *Modern Banking in India* (Bombay: New Book Company, 1940)

414. Naidu, B. V. N., 'The Nattukkottai Chettiars and their Banking System' in B. V. N. Naidu (ed.), *Rajah Sir Annamalai Chettiar Commemoration Volume* (Annamalai Nagar: Annamalai University, 1941)

415. Nanjundan, S., *Indians in the Malayan Economy* (Delhi: Publication Division, Government of India, 1949)

416. *Nattukkottai Chettiars' Association Memorandum before the Ceylon Banking Commission* Ceylon Sessional Paper XXVIII. Colombo 1934

417. Noel-Paton, Frederick, *Burma Rice* (Calcutta: Government Printing, 1912)

418. A Note on ' The Council of State-The Insurance Bill Debate ' *The Indian Annual Register* (Calcutta) Vol. II No. 20. July-December 1937

419. A Note on ' Trade and Finance-Federation of Indian Chambers' *The Indian Review* (Madras) Vol. XII. No. 3. March 1940

420. A Note on ' The Council of State-Debate on the Finance Bill: Limitation Act Amendment.' *The Indian Annual Register* (Calcutta) Vol. 1. No. 24. January–June 1941.

421. A note on ' Sterling Negotiations ' *Modern Review* (Calcutta) Vol. LXXXIV. No. 2. 1948

422. Odell, Francis David, *Market Surveys of Burma Crops* (Rangoon: Superintendent, Government Printing, 1936)

423. Office of the Economic Adviser, India, *Indians in Malayan Economy* (Delhi: Manager of Publications, 1950).

424. Ooi, Jin-bee, ' Rural Development in Tropical Areas with Special Reference to Malaya ' *Journal of Tropical Geography* (Singapore) 1959

425. ———, *Land, People and Economy in Malaya* See 126

426. Otto-Walter, Renate, ' Subsistenzproduktion and Produktionsweise die indische Diskussion ' Programme in Development Studies, Department of Sociology, University of Bielefeld, Bielefeld, 1978

427. Parker, H., ' The Rice Industry of Burma ' *The Malaysian Agricultural Journal* (Kuala Lumpur) Vol. XXIV. No. 3. March 1936

428. Pearn, B. R., ' The Commercial Treaty of 1862' *Journal of the Burma Research Society* (Rangoon) Vol. XXVII. January 1937.

429. Periplus Maris Erythraei, *The Periplus of the Erythrean Sea: Travel and Trade in the Indian Ocean, by a Merchant of the First Century* Translated from the Greek and annotated by Wilfred H. Schoot (New York: Longmans Green, 1912)

430. Pfanner, David E. and Jasper Ingersoll, ' Theravada Buddhism and Village Economic Behaviour ' *Journal of Asian Studies* (Durham) Vol. XII. May 1962

431. Pillai, P. P. (ed.), *Labour in South -East Asia, a Symposium* (New Delhi: Indian Council of World Affairs, 1947)

432. Planning Forum, *Socio Economic Survey of Pallathur, Ramanathapuram District* See 277.

433. Playne, Somerset, *Southern India: Its History, People, Commerce* and *Industrial Resources* See 224

434. Puthucheary, James, *Ownership and Control in the Malaysian Economy* (Singapore: Eastern University Press, 1961)

435. Rao, A. Narayan, *Indian Labour in Burma* (Madras: Kesari Printing Works, 1933)

436. Rao, K. M. Gururaja, 'A Brief Sketch of the Background for Agricultural Planning' *The Modern Review* (Calcutta) Vol. LXXIX. No. 3. March 1946

437. Rao, V. K. R. V., *The National Income of British India 1931-32* (London: Macmillan, 1940)

438. Rau, C. Hayavadana, 'The Banking Caste of South India' *Indian Review* (Madras) Vol. VIII. 1907

439. *Reports on the Trade and Customs of Burma, 1867-1875* (Rangoon: Superintendent, Government Printing, 1868-1876

440. *Reports on the Revenue Administration of British Burma, 1867-1935* (Rangoon: Government Press, 1868-1936)

441. *Reports of Maritime Trade and Customs, 1881-82* (Rangoon: Superintendent, Government Printing, 1882)

442. *Reports on the Trade and Navigation of Burma, 1875-1902* (Rangoon: Superintendent, Government Printing, 1876-1903)

443. *Reports on the Maritime Trade of Burma, 1902-1906* (Rangoon: Superintendent, Government Printing, 1903-1907)

444. *Reports on the Trade and Customs Administration of Burma, 1906-1937*, (Rangoon: Superintendent, Government Printing, 1907-1938)

445. Reports *on the Operations of the Department of Agriculture, 1906-1940* (Rangoon: Superintendent, Government Printing 1907-1941)

446. *Reports on the Land Revenue Administration of Burma During the Year ending the* 30th *June* 1914 (Rangoon: Superintendent Government Printing, 1915)

447. *Reports of the Committee on Financial Relations* Cmd. 724. (London: His Majesty's Stationery Office, 1920)

448. *Reports of the Committee on Burma Land Revenue System* (*Furnival Committee*) (Rangoon: Government Press, 1922)
449. *Reports on the Conditions of Agricultural Tenants and Labour in Burma* (Couper Committee) (Rangoon: Government Press, 1926)
450. *Reports of the Royal Commission on Agriculture in India* (Calcutta: Government of India, 1927)
451. *Reports on the standard and Cost of Living of the Working Classes in Rangoon* (Rangoon: Government Press, 1928)
452. *Report of the Royal Commission on Agriculture in India* Vol. XII (London: His Majesty's Stationery Office, 1928)
453. *Report of the State Mortgage Bank*, Sessional Paper XXI. (Colombo, 1929)
454. *Report of the Agricultural Finance Committee* (Rangoon: Government Press, 1930)
455. *Report of the Provincial Banking Enquiry Committee 1929-30 Banking and Credit in Burma* Vol I. (Rangoon: Superintendent, Government Printing, 1930)
456. *Report of the Madras Province Banking Enquiry Committee*, (Madras, 1930)
457. *Report of the Provincial Banking Enquiry Committee, Burma 1929-30* Vols. II and III. (Rangoon: Superintendent, Government Printing, 1930)
458. *Report of the Royal Commission on Labour in India* (Calcutta: Government of India, 1931)
459. *Report of the Select Committee of Relief to Debtors*, Sessional Paper III. (Colombo, 1932)
460. *Report of the Ceylon Banking Commission—Memoranda and Evidence* Vol. I. Sessional Paper XXII. (Colombo, 1934)
461. *Report of the Ceylon Banking Commission—Memoranda and Evidence* Vol. II. Sessional Paper XXIII. (Colombo, 1934)
462. *Report on the Land Revenue Administration of Burma During the year ending* 30th *June* 1934 (Rangoon: Superintendent, Government Printing, 1935)
463. *Report on the Land Revenue Administration of Burma During the Year ending* 30th *June* 1935 (Rangoon: Superintendent, Government Printing, 1936)

464. *Report on the Land Revenue Administration of Burma During the Year ending* 30th *June* 1936 (Rangoon: Superintendent, Government Printing, 1937)
465. *Report of the Rice Export Trade Enquiry Committee* (Rangoon: Superintendent, Government Printing, 1937)
466. *Reports on the Maritime Trade and Customs Administration of Burma*, 1906-1937 (Rangoon: Superintendent, Government Printing, 1907-1938)
467. *Report on the Land and Agriculture Committee—Tenancy* Part I (Rangoon: Superintendent, Government Printing, 1938)
468. *Report on the Land and Agriculture Committee—Land Alienation* Part II (Rangoon: Superintendent, Government Printing, 1938)
469. *Reports of the Burma Fiscal Committee, 1938–1939* (Rangoon: Government Press, 1938–1939)
470. *Reports on the Working of the Co-operative Societies Act in Burma 1905–1940* (Rangoon: Superintendent, Government Printing, 1906–1941)
471. *Reports on the Working of the Indian Factories Act in Burma, 1911–1940* (Rangoon: Superintendent, Government Printing, 1912–1941)
472. *Report on the Marketing of Rice in India and Burma* (Delhi: Government Press, 1941)
473. *Reports of the Burma Land and Agricultural Committee, 1938–40* (I-IV) (Rangoon: Government Press, 1938–1940)
474. *Report on the Land and Agriculture Committee – Agricultural Finance, Colonization and Land purchase* Part III (Rangoon: Superintendent, Government Printing, 1939)
475. *Report on the Land and Agriculture Committee—Regulation of Money-lending, Agricultural Finance* Part IV (Rangoon: Superintendent, Government Printing, 1939)
476. *Report of the Sub-Committee on Commercial Legislation*, Sessional Paper X. (Colombo, 1939)
477. *Report of the Committee on Expenditure on Public Services* (Rangoon: Government Press, 1940)
478. *Report of the Commission on Conditions of Indentured Labour* (Kuala Lumpur: Federated Malay States, 1910)

479. *Report of the Commission on Conditions of Indentured Labour* (Kuala Lumpur: Federated Malay States, 1911)
480. *Report on the Working of Co-operative Societies in Burma for the Year ending June 30, 1940.* (Rangoon: Superintendent, Government Printing, 1940)
481. *Report on the Development of Small-Scale and Cottage Industries in Burma* (New York: United Nations Technical Assistance Administration, 1952)
482. *Report on the Working of Co-operative Societies in the State of Madras for the Year Ending* 30*th June* 1960–62 (Madras, 1962)
483. Reshick, Stephen A., *A Socio-economic Inter-relation of the Decline of Rural Industry under Export Expansion: A Comparison Among Burma, Philippines and Thailand, 1870–1938* (New Haven: Yale University 1969)
484. Robertson, C. J., 'The Rice Export from Burma, Siam and French Indo-China' *Pacific Affairs* (New York) Vol. IX. No. 2. 1936
485. *Royal Commission of Agriculture in India and Burma* Vol. XII. (Rangoon: Superintendent, Government Printing, 1928)
486. Sadasivan, S. T., 'Three Hundred Years of Banking in Madras' Tercentenary Committee (ed.), *Madras Tercentenary Commemoration Volume* (Madras: Madras Tercentenary Committee, 1939)
487. Scott, James C., *The Rural Economy of the Peasant: Rebellion and Subsistence in South-East Asia* (New Haven: Yale University Press, 1976)
488. ———, *Burma: A Handbook of Practical, Commercial and Political Information* (London: Alexander Moring, 1921).
489. *Season and Crop Report* (Rangoon: Superintendent, Government Printing, 1910)
490. *Season and Crop Report* (Rangoon: Superintendent, Government Printing, 1914)
491. Selvaratnam, V., 'Indian Plantation Workers in West Malaysia' Paper presented at the Seminar on Indians Abroad: Asia and Africa, Kuala Lumpur, University of Malaya, 1969 (Mimeographed)
492. Sethuraman, V., *The Law of Sales Tax in India* (Madras: Southern Law House, 1953)

493. Shenoy, B. R., *Ceylon Currency and Banking* (London: Longmans, 1941)

494. Siegelman, Philip, 'Religion and Economic Activity: The Chettiars of Madras' Paper read at the Sixth Annual Meeting of the International Society for the Study of the Underdeveloped Economies, Washington, D.C. 1964

495. ———, 'Colonial Development and the Chettiar: A Study in Political Economic Ecology of Modern Burma' Unpublished Doctoral Dissertation, 1962, University of Minnesota. (Ann Arbor: Michigan University Microfilms International, 1976)

496. Siok-Hwa, Cheng, *The Rice Industry of Burma 1852–1940* (Kuala Lumpur: University of Malaya Press, 1968)

497. Slater, Gilbert (ed.), *Economic Studies: Some South Indian Villages* (Madras: Oxford University Press, 1918)

498. ———, *Southern India: Its Political and Economic Problems* (London: George Allen and Unwin, 1936)

499. Somalay, 'Chettiar Contribution to Commerce and Industry' *Journal of the Annamalai University* Silver Jubilee Volume (Annamalai Nagar: Annamalai Univesity, 1955)

500. Sovani, N. V., *Economic Relations of India with South-East Asia and the Far East* (New Delhi: Oxford University Press, 1949)

501. *Statements of the Sea-borne Trade and Navigation of Burma, 1855–1940.* (Rangoon: Superintendent, Government Printing 1856–1941)

502. Sundaram, Lanka, 'The Chettiars of Indo-China—An Economic Appraisal' *Modern Review* (Calcutta) Vol. LIV. No. 3. 1933

503. ———, *Indians Overseas: A Study of Economic Sociology* See 287.

504. Tamagna, F. M., *Banking and Finance in China* (New York: Institute of Pacific Relations, 1942)

505. Thomas, P. J., 'The Nattukkottai Chettiars—A Community of Bankers' *Journal of the Madras University* (Madras) Vol. V. 1933

506. ———, 'Nattukkottai Chettiars' in B. V. N. Naidu (ed.) *Rajah Sir Annamalai Chettiar Commemoration Volume* (Annamalai Nagar: Annamalai University, 1941)

507. Thompson, Virginia, *Labour Problems in South-East Asia* (New Haven: Yale University Press, 1947)
508. *Trade and Immigration Relations Between India and Burma After this Separation of Burma* Cmd. 4985 (London: His Majesty's Stationery Office, 1935)
509. Trager, Frank, N., 'Review of U Tun Wai: Burma's Currency and Credit' *Pacific Affairs* (New York) Vol. XXVII. December 1954
510. Tun Wai, U., *Burma's Currency and Credit* (Calcutta: Orient Longmans, 1953)
511. ———, *Economic Development of Burma from 1800 to 1940* (Rangoon: University of Rangoon, 1961)
512. Turner, L. J. B., *Population in Ceylon, Its History, People, Commerce Industries and Resources* See 186
513. Vaidyanathan, P., 'Problems of Rural Credit in Madras Presidency—Money-lending and Regulation of Money-lending' *Journal of the Annamalai University* (Annamalai Nagar) Vol. XI. 1941–42
514. ———, 'Problems of Rural Credit in Madras Presidency—Indigenous Banking' *Journal of the Annamalai University* (Annamalai Nagar) Vol. XI. 1941
515. Walinsky, L. J., *Economic Development in Burma*—1951–60 (New York: Twentieth Century Fund, 1962)
516. Weerasooria, W. S., *The Nattukkottai Chettiar: Merchant Bankers in Ceylon* (Delhiwala, Sri Lanka: Tisara Prakasakayo, 1973)
517. Wickizer, V. D. and M. K. Bennet, *Rice Economy of Monsoon Asia* (Stanford: Food Research Institute, 1941)
518. Wijesinghe, Mallory E., *The Economy of Sri Lanka: 1948–75* (Colombo: Ranco Printers and Publsishers, 1976)
519. Wong, David S. Y. *Tenure and Land Dealings in the Malay States* (Singapore: Singapore University Press, 1975)
520. Zimmerman, C. C., *Siam, Rural Economic Survey 1930–31* (Bangkok: Ministry of Commerce and Communications, 1931)

## 7. RELIGION AND TEMPLES

521. *Administration Report of the Elayathakudi Devasthanam* (Karaikudi: Chettinad Press, 1939)
522. Aiyer, V. G., Ramakrishna, *The Economy of a South Indian Temple* See 294
523. Arasaratnam, S., *Indian Festivals in Malaya* (Kuala Lumpur: The Department of Indian Studies, University of Malaya, 1966)
524. Bhattacharya, J. N., *Hindu Castes and Sects* See 251
525. Cady, F. John, 'Religion and Politics in Modern Burma' *The Far Eastern Quarterly* (U.S.A.) Vol. XII. February 1953
526. Census of India 1961, Madras *Temples of Madras State Chingleput District and Madras City* Part XI-D Vol. IX. (Madras: Government of India, 1965)
527. ———, *Temples of Madras State (ii) Tiruchirapalli and South Arcot* Part XI. Vol. IX. (Madras: Government of India, 1966)
528. ———, *Fairs and Festivals* Part VII-B. Vol. IX (Madras: Government of India, 1968)
529. ———, *Temples of Madras State (iii) Coimbatore and Salem* Part XI-D. Vol. IX. (Madras: Government of India, 1968)
530. ———, *Temples of Madras State (iv) North Arcot and Nilgiris* Part XI-D. Vol. IX. (Madras: Government of India, 1968)
531. ———, *Temples of Madras State (v) Kanyakumari and Tirunelveli* Part XI-D. Vol. IX. (Madras: Government of India, 1968)
532. Coomarasamy, A. K., *The Dance of Shiva* (Bombay: Asia Publishing House, 1948)
533. *Foundations by Thiagaraja Trusts, Madurai* (Madurai: Thiagaraja Trusts, 1966)
534. *A Full Report of the Proceedings of a Meeting held on* 6-1-1924 *at the Mariamman Temple, High Street, Kuala Lumpur to concert measures for the good Government of the Temple and its funds* (Kuala Lumpur, 1924)
535. Iddiakkadar, N. Manicka, 'Hindu Shrines of the Vanni' *Hindu Organ* Diamond Jubilee Number (Colombo) April 1950

536. Lahiri, Sisir Chandra, *Principles of Modern Burmese Buddhist Law* (Calcutta: Eastern Law House, 1951)
537. Mahadevan, T. M. P. *The Idea of God in Saiva Siddhanta* (Annamalai Nagar: Annamalai University, 1955)
538. Muthusamy, Damayanthi, *Sri Thandayudhapani Temple, Singapore* (Singapore: Univesity of Singapore, 1958) Unpublished Academic Exercise
539. Nagaswamy, R., 'Architecture in Tamil Nadu' *Journal of Tamil Studies* (Madras) Vol. 1. April 1969
540. Pfanner, David E. and Jasper Ingersoll, 'Theravada Buddhism and Village Economic Behaviour' See 430
541. Pillai, G. M. Muthuswamy, *Siva Cult and Heritage* (Mylapore: Saiva Siddhanta Maha Samajam, 1968)
542. Pillai, K.K., *The Suchindram Temple* (Madras: Kalakshetra Publications, 1953)
543. Rajamanickam, M., *The Development of Saivism in South India* (A.D. 300–1300) (Madras: University of Madras, 1964)
544. Rangasami, M.K. 'An Artistic Temple in Chettinad' *The Hindu* (Madras) 10 December 1967
545. Ray, Nihar-Ranjan, *Brahmanical Gods in Burma: A Chapter of Indian Art and Iconography* (Calcutta: Calcutta University Press 1932)
546. ———, *Sanskrit Buddhism in Burma* (Amsterdam: H.J. Paris, 1936)
547. Report of Seminars and Lectures, 'Chettiars and Hinduism in South-East Asia' *Bulletin of the Institute of the Traditional Cultures* (Madras) July-December 1972
548. Shivapadasundarm, S., *The Saiva School of Hinduism* (London: George Allen and Unwin, 1934)
549. Siegelaman, Philip, 'Religion and Economic Activity—The Chettiars of Madras' See 494
550. *Singapore Hindus' Religious and Cultural Seminar 1969–71* (Singapore: The Organising Committee, 1971)
551. Sivaratnam, C., *An Outline of the Cultural History and Principles of Hinduism* (Colombo: Standard Printer Ltd. 1964)
552. Somalay, 'Chettiars and Hinduism in South-East Asia' *Madras University Journal* (Madras 1972)

553. Somasundaram, J. M., *Tiruchendur—The Sea-shore Temple of Subramanya Commemoration Volume* (Thiruvaduthurai: Thiruvaduthurai Adinam, 1948).

554. Spencer, Robert (ed.), *Religion and Change in Contemporary Asia* (Minneapolis: The University of Minnesota Press, 1971)

## 8. EDUCATIONAL, RELIGIOUS AND OTHER BENEFACTIONS


555. *Administration Report of the Elayathakudi Devasthanam* See 521

556. Aiyar, P. A. Subramaniam, 'The Beginning of the Annamalai University' in B. V. N. Naidu (ed.), *Rajah Sir Annamalai Chettiar Commemoration Volume* (Annamalai Nagar: Annamali University, 1941)

557. Alagappa Chettiar Educational Trust, *Dr. Alagappa Educational Institutions, Karaikudi* Silver Jubilee Souvenir (Karaikudi: Alagappa Chettiar Educational Trust, 1973)

558. Arasaratnam, S., *Indian Festivals in Malaya* See 523.

559. Chakko, K. C., 'Annamalai University—Lands and Buildings' in B. V. N. Naidu (ed.), *Rajah Sir Annamalai Chettiar Commemoration Volume* (Annamalai Nagar: Annamalai University, 1941)

560. *Foundations by Thiagaraja Trusts, Madurai* See 533

561. *A Full Report of the Proceedings of a Metting held on* 6-1-1924 *at the Mariamman Temple, High Street, Kuala Lumpur to Concert Measures for the good Government of the Temple and its Funds* See 534

562. Iyer, P. S. Sivasamy, 'School Opening Ceremony Address' A Report in *Madras Mail* (Madras) 6 August 1916

563. Multum in Parvo—Notes 'Questions of Importance: Educational Benefactions' *The Indian Review* (Madras) Vol. XXXVI. No. 9. September 1935

564. A Note on 'The Madras Legislative Council—The Annamalai University Bill' *The Indian Quarterly Register* (Calcutta) Vol. II. Nos. III and IV. July-December 1928

565. Pillai, V. K. Ayappan, 'The Annamalai University—A Unique Foundation' in B. V. N. Naidu (ed.), *Rajah Sir Annamalai Chettiar Commemoration Volume* (Annamalai Nagar: Annamalai University, 1941)

566. Rangasami, M. K. 'An Artistic Temple in Chettinad' See 544

567. *Report of the Hindu Religious Endowments Commission* (New Delhi: Government of India, 1960–1962.)

568. Somasundaram, J. M., ' Annamalai University Celebrates Silver Jubilee ' See 104

## 9. LANGUAGE AND CULTURE

569. Aiyangar, S. Krishnasamy, *Some Contributions of South India to Indian Culture* See 1

570. Annamalai University, *Prof. T. P. Meenakshisundaram Sixty-First Birthday Commemoration Volume* (Annamalai Nagar: Annamalai University, 1961)

571. Chettiar, O. RM. M. SP. SV. AN. Annamalai, 'Tamil Culture in Malaysia' in N. Srinivasan *et al* (eds.) *Sree Sevugan Annamalai College Magazine* (Devakottai) Vol. VII. 1977

572. Chetty, Simon Casie, *Caste, Customs and Manners and Literature of the Tamils* See 256

573. Danielou, Alain, *Shilappadikaram* See 27

574. Dikshitar, V. R. R. *The Silappadikaram* See 29

575. Embree, John F. and Lillian O. Dotson, *Bibliography of the Peoples and Cultures of Mainland South-East Asia* (New Haven Yale University, South-East Asia Studies, 1950)

576. Gunasegaram, S. J. *Tamil Cultural Influences in South East Asia* (Colombo: Ceylon Private Ltd., 1958)

577. Jesudasan, C. and Hephzibah Jesudasan, *A History of Tamil Literature* (Calcutta: Y.M.C.A. Publishing House, 1961)

578. Kratoska, Paul H., 'The Chettiar and the Yeoman—British Cultural Categories and Rural Indebtedness in Malaya' An Occasional Paper of the Institute of South-East Asian Studies, Singapore, 1975

579. Le May, R., *The Culture of South-East Asia* (London: George Allen and Unwin, 1954)

580. Meenakshisundaram, T. P. *A History of Tamil Literature* (Annamalai Nagar: Annamalai University, 1965)

581. Ragavan, M. D. *The Tamils in Ceylon: India in Celyonese History, Society and Culture* See 225

582. Rajeswari A., 'Tamil Journalism and the Indian Community in Malaya 1920–1941' *Journal of Tamil Studies* (Madras) Vol. II. No. 2. October 1970

583. Secretary of Ramakrishna Mission (ed.) *The Cultural Heritage of India* See 100

584. *Singapore Hindus Religious and Cultural Seminar* 1969–71 See 550
585. Somasundaram, J. M. *Two Thousands Years of Tamil Literature* (Madras: The South India Saiva Siddhanta Works Publishing Society, 1959)
586. Tambiah, H. W., *Laws and Customs of the Tamils of Ceylon* (Colombo: Tamil Cultural Society of Ceylon, 1954)
587. Thaninayagam, Xavier S., *Nature and Landscape in Ancient Tamil Poetry* (Tuticorin: Tamil Literature Society, 1953)
588. Thinnappan, Sp. 'A Study of Kinship Terms in Chettiar Dialect' in Agesthialingom (ed.) *Collection of Papers presented in the Eighth Conference—Seminar* (Mysore: Central Institute of Indian Languages 1976)
589. ———, 'Nagarathar's Way of Letter Writing' Paper Presented in the Seminar on Socio-linguistics and Dialectology held under the auspices of the Centre of Advanced Study in Linguistics, Annamalai University, Annamalai Nagar, March 1977
590. Winstedt, R. O. *The Malaysian Cultural History* (London: Routledge and K. Paul, 1961)

## 10. BIOGRAPHIES AND PERSONALITIES

591. Adinarayan, S. P., *The Founder's Day Address* (Annamalai Nagar: Annamalai University, 1969)

592. ———, *Annual Convocation Address* (Annamalai Nagar: Annamalai University, 1975)

593. Aiyar, R. V. Krishna, *Annual Convocation Address* (Annamalai Nagar: Annamalai University, 1934)

594. Aiyar, K. V. Krishnaswami, *The Founder's Day Address* (Annamalai Nagar: Annamalai University, 1930)

595. Aiyar, K. Nagaraja, *The Founder's Day Address* (Annamalai Nagar: Annamalai University, 1976)

596. Aiyar, C. P. Ramaswami, *Annual Convocation Address* (Annamalai Nagar: Annamalai University, 1953)

597. ———, *The Founder's Day Address* (Annamalai Nagar: Annamalai University, 1964)

598. ———, *Annual Convocation Address* (Annamalai Nagar: Annamalai University, 1965)

599. Aiyar, P. A. Subhramanyam, ' Our Founder ' in B. V. N. Naidu (ed.), *Rajah Sir Annamalai Chettiar Commemoration Volume* (Annamalai Nagar: Annamalai University, 1941)

600. Aiyar, N. Ramaswami, *The Founder's Day Address* (Annamalai Nagar: Annamalai University, 1970)

601. Alagappa Chettiar Educational Trust, (ed.), *Dr. Alagappa Educational Institutions Silver Jubilee Souvenir* See 557

602. Ananthanarayanan, M., *The Founder's Day Address* (Annamalai Nagar: Annamalai University, 1967)

603. Annadurai, C. N., *Annual Convocation Address* (Annamalai Nagar: Annamalai University, 1967)

604. Arunachalam, M., ' The Life and Philosophy of the Siddhar Pattinattar ' *Saiva Siddhanta* (Madras) Vol. VIII. No. 2. September 1973

605. Bahadur, Abdul Hamid Sahib, *The Founder's Day Address* (Annamalai Nagar: Annamalai University, 1935)

606. Bahadur, Janab Basheer Ahmed Sayeed Sahib, *The Founder's Day Address* (Annamalai Nagar: Annamalai University, 1943)

607. Bahadur, Jaya Chamaraja Wadiyar, *Annual Convocation Address* (Annamalai Nagar: Annamalai University, 1964)
608. Bahadur, Khan Bahadur Sir Mahomed Usman Saheb, *Annual Convocation Address* (Annamalai Nagar: Annamalai University, 1941)
609. Bhaktavatsalam, M., *The Founder's Day Address* (Annamalai Nagar: Annamalai University, 1951)
610. ———, *Annual Convocation Address* (Annamalai Nagar: Annamalai University, 1963)
611. Bharati, Somasundara, ' The Rajah of Chettinad ' in B. V. N. Naidu (ed.), *Rajah Sir Annamalai Chettiar Commemoration Volume* (Annamalai Nagar: Annamalai University, 1941)
612. Bharathiar, Yogi Suddhanada, *The Founder's Day Address* (Annamalai Nagar: Cnnamalai University, 1951)
613. Chandrasekhar, S., *Annual Convocation Address* (Annamalai Nagar: Annamalai University, 1970)
614. Chavan, Y. B., *Annual Convocation Address* (Annamalai Nagar: Annamalai University, 1976)
615. Chettiar, T. S. Avinasilingam, *Annual Convocation Address* (Annamalai Nagar: Annamalai University, 1946)
616. Chettiar, Rajah Sir Muthiah, *Annual Convocation Address* (Annamalai Nagar: Annamalai University, 1974)
617. Chetty, R. K. Shanmukham, *The Founder's Day Address* (Annamalai Nagar: Annamalai University, 1940)
618. ———, *Annual Convocation Address* (Annamalai Nagar: Annamalai University, 1943)
619. Damodaran, M. P., *et al* (eds.), *Kumara Rajah M. A. M. Muthiah Chettiar Souvenir* (Madras: Memorial Committee, 1971)
620. Deshmukh, C. D., *Annual Convocation Address* (Annamalai Nagar: Annamalai University, 1957)
621. Desikachari, T., *Annual Convocation Address* (Annamalai Nagar: Annamalai University, 1933)
622. Galbraith, John Kenneth, *Annual Convocation Address* (Annamalai Nagar: Annamalai University, 1961)
623. Gownder, K. Ramaswami, *The Founder's Day Address* (Annamalai Nagar: Annamalai University, 1955)

624. Hidayatullah, M., *Annual Convocation Address* (Annamalai Nagar: Annamalai University, 1967)
625. Ismail, M. M., *The Founder's Day Address* (Annamalai Nagar: Annamalai Univcrsity, 1975)
626. Ismail Mirza, *Annual Convocation Address* (Annamalai Nagar: Annamalai University, 1935)
627. Iyer, S. Ramachandra, *The Founder's Day Address* (Annamalai Nagar: Annamalai University, 1963)
628. Jesudasan, C. and Hephzibah Jesudasan, *A History of Tamil Literature* See 577
629. Kabir, Humayun, *Annual Convocation Address* (Annamalai Nagar: Annamalai University, 1958)
630. Kailasam, P. S., *The Founder's Day Address* (Annamalai Nagar: Annamalai University, 1962)
631. Krishnamachari, T. T., *The Founder's Day Address* (Annamalai Nagar: Annamalai University, 1939)
632. Leach, Lionel, *Annual Convocation Address* (Annamalai Nagar: Annamalai University, 1940)
633. Littlehailes, R., *Annual Convocation Address* (Annamalai Nagar: Annamalai University, 1932)
634. ———, *The Founder's Day Address* (Annamalai Nagar: Annamalai University, 1934)
635. Mack, E. E. *The Founder's Day Address* (Annamalai Nagar: Annamalai University, 1954)
636. Maharaja of Travancore, *Annual Convocation Address* (Annamalai Nagar: Annamalai University, 1942)
637. Maharajan, S., *The Founder's Day Address* (Annamalai Nagar: Annamalai University, 1972)
638. Manickavelu, M. A. *The Founder's Day Address* (Annamalai Nagar: Annamalai University, 1957)
639. Master, M. A., *The Founder's Day Address* (Annamalai Nagar: Annamalai University, 1946)
640. Medhi, Bishnuram, *Annual Convocation Address* (Annamalai Nagar: Annamali University, 1962)
641. Meenakshisundaram, T. P., *A History of Tamil Literature* See 580
642. Menon, P. Govinda, *The Founder's Day Address* (Annamalai Nagar: Annamalai University, 1953)

643. Menon, K. Madhava, *Annual Convocation Address* (Annamalai Nagar: Annamalai University, 1950)

644. Menon, K. P. S. *Many Worlds: An Autobiography* (London: Oxford University Press, 1966)

645. Mudaliar, A. Lakshamanaswami, *The Founder's Day Address* (Annamalai Nagar: Annamalai University, 1943)

646. ———, *Annual Convocation Address* (Annamalai Nagar: Annamalai University, 1954)

647. Mudaliar, C. P., 'Rajah Sir Annamalai Chettiar, Savant and Patron of Tamil Literature' in B. V. N. Naidu (ed.), *Rajah Sir Annamalai Chettiar Commemoration Volume* (Annamalai Nagar: Annamalai University, 1941)

648. Mudaliar, C. S., Ratnasabhapati, *The Founder's Day Address* (Annamalai Nagar: Annamalai University, 1944)

649. Multum in Parvo—Notes 'A Portrait of Sir Muthiah' *The Indian Review* (Madras) Vol. XLI. No. 10. October 1940

650. Naidu, S. Ramaswami, *The Founder's Day Address* (Annamala. Nagar: Annamalai University, 1949)

651. Naidu, T. Sundara Rau, *The Founder's Day Address* (Annamalai Nagar: Annamalai University, 1947)

652. Natarajan, K., *Annual Convocation Address* (Annamalai Nagar: Annamalai University, 1938)

653. Nedunchezhiyan, V. R. *The Founder's Day Address* (Annamalai Nagar: Annamalai University, 1967)

654. A Note on 'Annamalai Chettiar, S. A. A.' in Chakravarthi Co. (ed.) *Almanack and Directory* (Madras: Asylum Press, 1930)

655. A Note on 'Aviation - Mr. Avadiappa Chettiar's First Flight Over Yomas' *The Indian Review* (Madras) Vol. 34. No. 1. January 1934

656. A Note on 'Kasi Chettiar, RM.' in Chakravarthi Co. (ed.) *Almanack and Directory* (Madras: Asylum Press, 1930)

657. A Note on 'Kasinathan Chettiar, C. A. C.' in Chakravarthi Co. (ed.), *Almanack and Directory* (Madras: Asylum Press, 1930)

658. A Note on ' Letchman Chettiar, Rao Bahadur, O. A. O. K.' in Chakravarthi Co. (ed.) *Almanack and Directory* (Madras: Asylum Press, 1930)

659. A Note on ' Narayanan Chettiar, AL. AR.' M.L.C., in Chakravarthi Co. (ed.), *Almanack and Directory* (Madras: Asylum Press, 1930)

660. A Note on 'Somanathan Chettiar' in Chakravarthi Co. (ed.), *Almanack and Directory* (Madras: Asylum Press, 1930)

661. A Note on ' Somasundarm Chettiar, Diwan Bahadur ' in Chakravarthi Co. (ed.), *Almanack and Directory* (Madras: Asylum Press, 1930)

662. A Note on ' Chettiar, Hon. Rajah Sir Annamalai Chettiar of Chettinad ' in Stanley Read and Francis Low. (eds.), *The Indian Year Book and Who's Who* (Bombay: Bennett Coleman and Co., 1938)

663. A Note on ' Chidambaram Chettiar, M. CT. M. ' in Stanley Read and Francis Low (eds.), *The Indian Year Book and Who's Who* (Bombay: Bennett Coleman and Co., 1938)

664. A Note on ' Who's Who in India—Kumararajah Sir Muthiah Annamalai Muthiah Chettiar of Chettinad, B. A. Kt. ' in Francis Low (ed.), *The Indian Year Book* Vol. XXXI. No. 31 (Bombay: Bennett Coleman and Co., 1945)

665. A Note on ' Arunachalam, A. M. M. ' in Francis Low (ed.), *The Madras Directory and Who's Who Section V* (Madras: Commercial Printing and Publishing House, 1946)

666. A Note on ' Murugappa Chettiar, A. M. M.' in Francis Low (ed.) *The Madras Directory and Who's Who Section V* (Madras: Commercial Printing and Publishing House, 1946)

667. A Note on ' Ramanathan Chettiar, S. RM.' in Francis Low (ed.), *The Madras Directory and Who's Who Section V* (Madras: Commercial and Publishing House, 1946)

668. A Note on ' Annamalai Chettiar ' *Modern Review* (Calcutta) Vol. LXXXIV. No. 1. July 1948

669. A Note on ' Chettiar, Dr. R. M. Alagappa ' in I.S. Jehu (ed.), *The Indian and Pakistan Year Book and Who's Who* (Bombay: Bennett Coleman and Co., 1949)

670. A Note on ' Chettiar, AL. VR. PV. VR. Veerappa ' in I.S. Jehu (ed)., *The Indian and Pakistan Year Book and Who's Who* (Bombay: Bennett Coleman and Co., 1949)

671. Papworth, H.C. *Annual Convocation Address* (Annamalai Nagar: Annamalai University, 1939)

672. Pavate, D. C. *Annual Convocation Address* (Annamalai Nagar: Annamalai University, 1969)

673. Pillai, J. Sivashanmugam, *The Founder's Day Address* (Annamalai Nagar: Annamalai University, 1948)

674. Pillai, S. Ganapathia, *The Founder's Day Address* (Annamalai Nagar: Annamalai University, 1958)

675. Pillai, T. M. N., *The Founder's Day Address* (Annamalai Nagar: Annamalai University, 1945)

676. ———, *Annual Convocation Address* (Annamalai Nagar: Annamalai University, 1956)

677. Prakasa, Sri, *Annual Convocation Address* (Annamalai Nagar: Annamalai University, 1952)

678. Raja, P. S. Kumaraswamy, *Annual Convocation Address* (Annamalai Nagar: Annamalai University, 1949)

679. Rajagopalan, P., *The Founder's Day Address* (Annamalai Nagar: Annamalai University, 1956)

680. Rajamannar, P. V., *Annual Convocation Address* (Annamalai Nagar: Annamalai University., 1948)

681. Rao, N. S. Subba, *The Founder's Day Address* (Annamalai Nagar: Annamalai University, 1937)

682. Rao, M. Venkatasubba, *The Founder's Day Address* (Annamalai Nagar: Annamalai University, 1938)

683. Reddi, B. Gopala, *Annual Convocation Address* (Annamalai Nagar: Annamalai University, 1951)

684. Reddi, Brahmananda, *Annual Convocation Address* (Annamalai Nagar: Annamalai University, 1976)

685. Reddiar, O. P. Ramaswami, *Annual Convocation Address* (Annamalai Nagar: Annamalai University, 1947)

686. Reddy, P. Chandra, *The Founder's Day Address* (Annamalai Nagar: Annamalai University, 1965)

687. Runganadhan, S. E., *Annual Convocation Address* (Annamalai Nagar: Annamalai University, 1931)

688. Ruthnaswami, M., *The Founder's Day Address* (Annamalai Nagar: Annamalai University, 1941)
689. Saheb, P. Janab Kalifullah, *Annual Convocation Address* (Annamalai Nagar: Annamalai University, 1944)
690. Sastri, V. S. Srinivasa, *Annual Convocation Address* (Annamalai Nagar: Annamalai Univesity, 1937)
691. Sastri, T. R. Venkatarama, *The Founder's Day Address* (Annamalai Nagar: Annamalai University, 1936)
692. Satyamurthi, S., *The Founder's Day Address* (Annamalai Nagar: Annamalai University, 1932)
693. Sethna, C. Phiroze, *Annual Convocation Address* (Annamalai Nagar: Annamalai University, 1936)
694. Shah, K. K. *Annual Convocation Address* (Annamalai Nagar: Annamalai University, 1973)
695. Somasundaram, J. M., *Two Thousand Years of Tamil Literature* See 585
696. Srinivasachariar, C. S. *The Founder's Day Address* (Annamalai Nagar: Annamalai University, 1933)
697. Staff of Chettinad Corporation (ed.), *Souvenir to Commemorate the Sixtieth Birthday* (*Shastiyabdha Poorthi of Sri SM. SP. Sockalingam Chettiar* (Colombo: Staff of Chettinad Corporation, 1957)
698. Strathie, Norman, *Annual Convocation Address* (Annamalai Nagar: Annamalai University, 1945)
699. Subbarayan, P., *The Founder's Day Address* (Annamalai Nagar: Annamalai University, 1952)
700. ———*Annual Convocation Address* (Annamalai Nagar: Annamalai University, 1960)
701. Subramaniam, C., *Annual Convocation Address* (Annamalai Nagar: Annamalai University, 1955)
702. Thacker, M. S. *Annual Convocation Address* (Annamalai Nagar: Annamalai University, 1958)
703. Thiagarajan, Karumuthu, *The Founder's Day Address* (Annamalai Nagar: Annamalai University, 1960)
704. Thiagarajan, Radha, *The Founder's Day Address* (Annamalai Nagar: Annamalai University, 1973)
705. Thiraviyam, K., *The Founder's Day Address* (Annamalai Nagar: Annamalai University, 1937)

706. Veeraswami, K., *The Founder's Day Address* (Annamalai Nagar: Annamalai University, 1961)
707. Venkataraman, R., *The Founder's Day Address* (Annamalai Nagar: Annamalai University, 1959)
708. Visveswarayya, M., *The Founder's Day Address* (Annamalai Nagar: Annamalai University, 1931)

## 11. LAW CASES

709. *Abeydeera* v *Ramanathan Chetty* (1936) 38 N.L.R. 389
710. *Achi* v *Palaniappa Chettiar* (1941) 42 N.L.R. 415
711. *Adaicappa Chetty* v *Thomas Cook & Sons* (1930) 31 N.L.R. 385
712. *Adaikalavan Chettiar* v *Kadiresan Chettiar* 8 P.L.R. 226
713. *Adaikappa Chetty* v *Letchuman Chetty* (1939) 40 N.L.R. 49
714. *Alagammai* v *Veerappa Chettiar* (1956) A.M. 428
715. *Alagammai Achi* v *Palaniappa Chettiar* (1940) 1 Mad. L.J.469
716. *Alagappa Chettiar* v *Vellayan Chettiar* I.L.R. 18 Madras 33
717. *Alagappa Chetty* v *Palaniappa Chetty* (1940) 42 N.L.R. 47
718. *Alagappa Chetty* v *Walker* (1885) 7 S.C.C. 18
719. *Alles* v *Palaniappa Chetty* (1917) 19 N.L.R. 334
720. *Amido Lebbe* v *Rasa Marcar* (1859) 3 Lorensz Rep. 155
721. *Anees* v *The Bank of Chettinad Ltd.* (1941) 42 N.L.R. 436
722. *Annamalai* v *Murugesan Chettiar* I.L.R. 26 Madras 544, 553
723. *Annamalai* v *Muthuswami* (1939) I.L.R. Madras 891
724. *Annamalai* v *Perumayi Ammal* (1965) A.M. 139, 141
725. *Annamalai Chetti* v *Annamalai Chetti* (1919) 52 I.C. 456
726. *Annamalai Chettiar* v *Annamalai Chettiar* 10 Law Weekly 175
727. *Annamalai Chettiar* v *Arunachalam Chettiar* 15 P.L.R. 176
728. *Annamalai Chettiar* v *Subramanian Chettiar* (1929) 31 B.L.R. 280-113 Indian Cases 897
729. *Annamalai Chetty* v *Lutchman Chetty* (1916) 36 I.C. 497
730. *Annamalai Chetty* v *Menaka* (1918) 20 N.L.R. 40 (F.B.)
731. *Annamalai Chetty* v *Thornhill* (1927) 29 N.L.R. 225
732. *Annamalai Chetty* v *Subramaniam Chetty* (1929) A.I.R.P.C.1.
733. *Annamalai Chetty* v *Thornhill* (1935) 36 N.L.R. 413
734. *Arnolis Appau in re Insolvency* (1917) 19 N.L.R. 478
735. *Arumugham* v *Valliammal* (1969) A.M. 72
736. *Arumugham Chettiar* v *Muthu* (1919) I.L.R. 42 Madras 711 52 I.C. 525
737. *Arumugham Chettiar* v *Ranganathan Chettiar* (1934) I.L.R. 57 Madras 405
738. *Arunachala* v *Arumugam* (1953) A.M. 550
739. *Arunachala* v *Virappa* 27 Madras 654
740. *Arunachalam Chettiar* v *Ramanathan Chettiar* (1935) 37 N.L.R. 263

741. *Arunachalam Chettiar* v *Valliappa* 27 M.L.J. 654
742. *Arunachalam Chettiar* v *Vyravan Chettiar* 57 M.L.J. 628 (P.C.)
743. *Arunasalam Chettiar* v *Arunasalam Chettiar* (1934) 37 N.L.R. 49
744. *Arunasalam Chetty* v *Bilinda* (1922) 1 Times Law Rep. 68
745. *Arunasalam Chettiar* v *Sokalingam Chettiar* (1933) 7 M.L.J. 137
746 *Arunasalam Chetty* v *Muthiah Chetty* (1918) 5 C.W.R. 152
747. *Arunasalam Chetty* v *Somasundaram Chetty* (1918) 20 N.L.R. 321
748. *Arunasalam Chetty* v *Somasundaram Chetty* (1920) 21 N.L.R. 389 (P.C.)
749. *Arunasalam Chetty* v *Somasundaram Chetty* (1921) 22 N.L.R. 281 (P.C.)
750. *Arunasalam Chetty* v *Wilson* (1929) 31 N.L.R. 213
751. *Attorney-General* v *Thirpooree Soonderee* (1874) 1 Ky. 377
752. *Attorney-General* v *Valliammai Atchie* (1949) 51 N.L.R. 169
753. *Attorney-General* v *Ramaswami Iyengar* (1953) 55 N.L.R. 496
754. *Attorney General* v *Arunasalam Chettiar* (1957) 59 N.L.R. 49 (P.C).
755. *The Bank of Bengal* v *K. P. Ramanathan Chetty* (1915) M.W.N. 180
756. *Bank of Chettinad Ltd.* v *Goonetilleka* (1936) 16 C.L.R. 13
757. *Bank of Chettinad Ltd.* v *Municipal Council of Colombo* (1954) 55 N.L.R. 361
758. *Bank of Chettinad Ltd.* v *Pulmadan Chetty* (1931) 33 N.L.R. 358
759. *Bank of Chettinad Ltd.* v *Tambiah* (1933) 35 N.L.R. 190
760. *Bank of Chettinad Ltd.* v *The Commissioner of Income Tax* (1948) 49 N.L.R. 409 (P.C.)
761. *Bank of Chettinad Ltd.* v *The Export Controller* (1935) 37 N.L.R. 190
762. *Bank of Madras* v *Sidembaram Chetty* (1883) 6 S.C.C. 153
763. *Bank of Madras* v *Virappa Chetty* (1880) 3 S.C.C. 138
764. *Bank of Madras* v *Weerappa Chetty* (1881) 4 S.C.C. 69
765. *Bank of Madras* v *Weerappa Chetty* (1885) 7 S.C.C. 89
766. *Bhagwandas Bagla* v *S. P. K. A . A. Chettiar firm* A.I.R. 1933 Rangoon 385
767. *Bhoy* v *Ramanathan Chetty* (1920) Indian Appeals 3
768. *Bhoy Hong Kong* v *Ramanathan Chetty* 29 I.A. 43, 48
769. *C. V. C. Chetty* v *P L. V. Chetty* (1972) A.M. 253

770. *Carpen Chetty* v *Connally* (1881) 4 S.C.C. 33
771. *Caruppen Chettiar* v *Wickremasekera* (1941) 6 C.L.J. 122
772. *Chartered Bank of India, Australia and China* v *Palaniappa Chetty* (1917) 19 N.L.R. 417
773. *Chartered Mercantile Bank of India, London and China* v *Sadayappa Chetty* (1887) 9 S.C.C. 80
774. *Chellammal* v *Ranganatha Pillai* I.L.R. 34 Madras 277
775. *Chellappa Chettiar* v *Annaamali Chettiar* 5 P.L.R. 232
776. *Chellappa Chettiar* v *Annamalai Chettiar* 5 P.L.R. 252
777. *Chithambaram Chettiar* v *Loo Khon Poo* and *Sinniah Chettiar* v *Puan Ying* (1940) M.L.J. 31, P.C.
778. *Chettinad Corporation Ltd.* v *Fernando* (1946) 48 N.L.R. 1
779. *Chettinad Corporation* v *Gamage* (1960) 62 N.L.R. 86
780. *Chettinad Corporation* v *Raman Chettiar* (1937) 10 C.L.W. 58
781. *Chetty* v *Chetty* (1935) 37 N.L.R. 253
782. *Chidambaram* v *Ramasami* 27 Mad. L.J. 631
783. *Chinniah Chettyar* v *Sivakami* (1945) A.M. 21
784. *Chinniah Chetty* v *Ramasami Chetty* (1915) 31 I.C. 317
785. *Commissioner of Income-Tax* v *Arunachalam Chettiar* (1935) 37 N.L.R. 145
786. *Commissioner of Income-Tax* v*P.K. N.* (1935) 37 N.L.R. 339
787. *Commissioner of Income-Tax* v *The Bank of Chettinad* (1946) 47 N.L.R. 25
788. *Coomarapah Chetty* v *Kang Oon Lock* 1 Ky. 314
789. *Courts Inspector* v *Murugappa Chetty* (1939) 3 C.L.J. 280
790. *Deivanai* v *Chidambaram Chettiar* (1954) A.I.R. Madras 657
791. *De Silva* v *Vaduganathan* (1926) 28 N.L.R. 337
792. *Dewasundera* v *Letchuman Chetty* (1933) 4 C.L.W. 112
793. *Dharmalingam Chetti* v *Vadivel Chetty* (1937) 2 C.L.J. 117
794. *Duncan Anderson & Co. in re* (1870) 3 N.L.R. 282
795. *Dyson* v *Kadiresan Chetty* (1928) 30 N.L.R. 216
796. *Evart* v *Chellamma* (1919) 21 N.L.R. 1
797. *Firm of R. M. K. R. M.* v *The Firm of M. R. M. V. L. R. M. K. R.M. Somasundaram Chetty* (1926) L.R. App Cas 761
798. *Firm of R.M.K.R.M.* v *Firm of M.R.M.V.L.* (1926) A.C.761, 763-4
799. *Firm Sadasuk Janki Das* v *Sir Kishen Parsad and Another* (1918) A.I.R. (P.C.) 146

800. *The Firm of T.AR.CT.* v *The Firm of SV.KR.* (1955) M.L.J.2 (P.C.)
801. *Ghulam Ravuthar* v *Viswanathan Chettiar* 40 I.C. 347
802. *Hull Blyth &Co.* v *Valliappa Chettiar* (1937) 39 N.L.R. 47
803. *Ismail* v *Muthiah Chettiar* (1942) 43 N.L.R. 450
804. *Jamal Mohideen & Co.* v *Meera Saibo* (1920) 22 N.L.R. 268
805. *Jayasinghe* v *Ramanathan Chettiar* (1948) 50 N.L.R. 546
806. *Jeevanjee* v *Muthiah Chetty* (1916) 3 Ceylon Weekly Reporter 220
807. *K.M.P.R.N.M. Firm* v *M. Somasundaram Chetty* I.L.R. 48 Madras 275; A.I.R. 1925 Madras 161
808. *K. S. RM. Chettiar* v *A. T. K. P. L.* I.L.R. 12 Rangoon 7
809. *Kadirkama Chetty* v *Ramanayake* (1919) 6 Ceylon Weekly Reporter 107
810. *Kandasamy* v *Sandaranayake* (1947) 48 N.L.R. 449
811. *Kannappa Chetty* v *Sundaram Pillai* (1909) 1 Current Law Reports 69
812. *Kannappa Chetty* v *Walathappa Chetty* (1903) 7 N.L.R. 339
813. *Karena Seyed Meyedin* v *Komarappa Chetty* (1909) 11 Straits Settlements Law Reports 70
814. *Karuppan Chetty* v *Fowler* (1905) 2 Balasingham Reports 73
815. *Karuppan Chetty* v *Palaniappa Chetty* (1907) 10 N.L.R. 228
816. *Karuppan Chetty* v *Harrison & Crossfield Ltd.* (1922) 24 N.L.R. 317
817. *Karuthan Chettiar* v *Chidambaram Chettiar* (1938) 2 Mad. L.J.79
818. *Kathiresan Chetty* v *Natchiappa Chetty* (1928) 30 N.L.R. 61
819. *Khan.* v *Muthiah Chetty* (1881) 4 S.C.C. 111
820. *King* v *Silva* (1923) 24 N.L.R. 493
821. *Krishnappa Chetty* v *Horatala* (1923) 29 N.L.R. 124
822. *Kutta Perumal Chetty* v *Martin* (1882) 5 S.C.C. 33
823. *Lakshmanan Chettiar* v *Commissioner of Income-Tax Madras* (1929) A.I.R. 675
824. *Lakshmanan Chettiar* v *Muthiah Chettiar* (1948) 50 N.L.R. 48
825. *Letchemenan Chetty* v *Mohamed Lebbe Marikar* (1885) 7 S.C.C. 168
826. *Letchimanan Chetty* v *Municipal Council, Colombo* (1942) 42 N.L.R 170

827. *Letchimanan Chetty* v *Murugappa Chetty* (1936) 39 N.L.R. 19
828. *Letchimanan Chetty* v *Perera* (1881) 4 S.C.C. 80
829. *Letchimanan Chetty* v *Sanmugam* (1903) 8 N.L.R. 121
830. *Letchiman Chetty* v *Periacarpen Chetty* (1879) 2 S.C.C. 193
831. *Manickam Chettiar, S.* v *Income-Tax Officer, Circle I* (3) *Karaikudi* The Income-Tax Reports (Madras) Vol. 104. Part 6. 9 August 1976
832. *Manigar of Pachilapali* v *Raman Chetty and Another* (1909) I Current Law Reports 64
833. *Manikka* v *Arunachala* (1965) A.M.P.I. (F.B.)
834. *Marcelin Perera* v *Sockalingam Chetty* (1946) 47 N.L.R. 265
835. *Marikar* v *Suppramaniam Chettiar* (1943) 44 N.L.R. 409 (F.B.).
836. *Mayappa Chetty* v *Usoof* (1902) 5 N.L.R. 265
837. *Medhankara Istawira* v *Suppramanian Chetty* (1939) 41 N.L.R. 327
838. *Meenachi Achi* v *The Firm of S.P.S.* 2 M.C. 212. C.A
839. *Megappan Chetty* v *Ramanathan* (1913) 16 N.L.R. 33
840. *Meiappan Chetty* v *Ramasamy Chettiar* (1939) 41 N.L.R. 327
841. *Mercantile Bank of India Ltd.* v *Ramanathan Chetty* (1937) 39 N.L.R. 448
842. *Meyappa Chetty* v *Khoo Bean Teen* 1 Ky. 510
843. *Meyappa Chetty* v *Ong Hong Pee* 4 Ky. 399
844. *Meyappan Chetty* v *Manchanayake* (1961) 62 N.L.R. 529
845. *Meyappan Chetty* v *Ramanathan* (1913) 16 N.L.R. 33
846. *Mohamado* v *Lapaya* (1913) 4 Balasingham Notes 11
847. *Mohamadu Cassim* v *Perianen Chetty* (1911) 14 N.L.R. 385
848. *Mohideen* v *S. A. P. N. Subramanian Chettiar* (1937) 2 Ceylon Law Journal 70
849. *Moragappa Chetty* v *Omar Lebba Marikar* (1875–76) Ramanathan Reports 100
850. *Moty* v *Kaylayan Chetty* (1931) 33 N.L.R. 182
851. *Murugappa Chetty* v *Ramantathan Chetty* (1935) 157 I.C. 274, 276
852. *Murugappa Chetti* v *S. Seenivasagam* (1936) M.L.J. 217 also (1940) M.L.J. 217 (C.A.)
853. *Murugappa Chettiar* v *Commissioner of Stamps* (1922) 24 N.L.R. 231
854. *Murugappa Chettiar* v *Krishnappa Chettiar* (1940) 9 M.L.J. 200

855. *Murugappa Chettiar* v *Muththal Achy* (1956) 58 N.L.R. 25 (P.C.)
856. *Murugappa Chettiar* v *Nagappa Chettiar* I.L.R. 29 Madras 161
857. *Murugappa Chettiar* v *Ramanathan Chettiar* (1937) 39 N.L.R. 231
858. *Murugesan* v *Manickavasagam* 44 I.A. 98
859. *Murugiah* v *Bastian Fernando* (1934) 11 Times Law Reports 193
860. *Muthappa Chetty* v *Yegappa Chetty* (1886) 7 S.C.C. 198
861. *Muthiah* v *Ramanathan* 43 Indian Cases 972
862. *Muthiah Chettiar, M. CT. Family Trust* v *4th Income-Tax Officer, City Circle VI, Madras* The Income-tax Reports (Madras) Vol. 86. 1972
863. *Muthiah Chettiar* v *Periannan Chettiar* 4 L.W. 228. Also 34 Indian Cases 551
864. *Muththal Achy* v *Murugappa Chettiar* (1954) 57 N.L.R. 27
865. *Muthu Carpen Chetty* v *Forbes Capper* (1881) 1 Ceylon Law Reports 10
866. *Muthukaruppa* v *Ramasami* 40 Madras 285.
867. *Muthukaruppa Chettiar* v *Sellathammal* I. L. R. 39 Madras 298
868. *Muthukaruppan Chetty* v *Abdul Hamid* (1910) 2 Current Law Reports 210
869. *Muthukaruppan Chetty* v *Salim* (1938) 3 Ceylon Law Journal 217
870. *Muthukumaran Chetty In re the Application of* (1917) 4 Ceylon Weekly Reporter 330
871. *Muthu Mohamadu* v *Ramaswamy Chetty* (1932) 33 N.L.R. 57
872. *Muthuraman* v *Periannan* (1934) A.I.R. Madras 62
873. *Muthu Raman Chetty* v *Kumarappan Chettiar* (1941) 43 N.L.R. 499
874. *Muthuraman Chetty* v *Perianan Chetty* (1934) A.I.R. Madras 621, 622
875. *Muthu Raman Chetty* v *Piper* (1890) 2 Balasingham Reports 174
876. *Muthu Raman Chetty* v *Sivasuppramaniam Chetty* (1909) 1 Current Law Reports 64
877. *Mayandan Brothers* v *Arunachalam Chetti* (1926) Madras 1106
878. *N. R. M. Chettiar* v *Darley Butler & Company* (1932) 34 N. L. R. 41
879. *Nachiappa* v *Muthukaruppa* (1946) Madras 858

880. *Nagamma Achi* v *Lakshmanan Chetty* (1957) 58 N.L.R. 481
881. *Narayanan Chetty* v *James Finlay & Co.* (1927) 29 N.L.R.
882. *Narayanan Chetty* v *Stevenson & Sons* (1881) 4 S.C.C. 2
883. *Narayanan Chetty* v *Suppiah Chetty* I.L.R. 43 Madras 629
884. *Narayanaswamy Chetty* v *Arnachella Chitty* (1862–63) 1 M. H.C.R (appendix) 487
885. *Nataraja* v *Kailasam* 44 Madras 283
886. *Natarajan Chettiar* v *Income-Tax Officer* The Income-Tax Reports (Madras) Vol. 42. 1961
887. *Noorbhai* v *Karuppan Chetty* (1925) 27 N.L.R. 325 (P.C.)
888. *Official Assignee* v *Ramaswami Chettiar* 43 Madras 747
889. *Official Assignee of Madras* v *Palaniappa Chetty* (1918) 41 Madras 824
890. *P. K. N. Kadappa Chettiar* v *A. R. M. Raman Chettiar* (1926) 8 Ceylon Law Recorder 42
891. *Palaniappa* v *Alagan* I.L.R. 44 Madras 740
892. *Palaniappa* v *Shanmugam* 41 Madras 815
893. *Palaniappa Chettiar* v *Alayan Chetti* (1921) 48. I.A. 539, 548
894. *Palaniappa Chettiar* v *Chokkalingam Chettiar* 57 M.L.J. 817
895. *Palaniappa Chettiar* v *Chop Nam Kee* (1913) 13 Straits Settlements Law Reports 6
896. *Palaniappa Chettiar* v *Hassan* (1939) 40 N.L.R. 409
897. *Palaniappa Chettiar* v *Mercantile Bank Ltd.* (1942) 43 N.L.R. 121, 127, 312
898. *Palaniappa Chettiar* v *Robert* (1923) 2 Times Law Reports 97
899. *Palaniappa Chetty* v *Deivasikamony* (1917) 44 I.A. 147, 155
900. *Palaniappa Chetty* v *de jong* (1913) 16 N.L.R. 271
901. *Paliamappar Chetty* v *Ploss Pol* (1907) 3 Balasingham Reports 102
902. *Palmadan Chetty* v *Bank of Chettinad* (1929) 33 N.L.R. 358
903. *Peria Carpen Chetty* v *Herft* (1880) 7 S.C.C. 182
904. *Peria Carpen Chetty* v *Perera* (1888) 8 S.C.C. 180
905. *Periya Karuppan Chettiar* v *The Commissioner of Stamps* (1936) 38 N.L.R. 20
906. *Pethachi Chettiar* v *Sangiliveeran* 10 Madras 241
907. *Pethaperumal* v *Muniyandi* 35 Ind. App. 98
908. *Pethaperumal Chettiar* v *C.I.T.* (1929) A.I.R. Madras 34
909. *Pettachi Chetty* v *Mohamado Yusoof* (1883) 6 N.L.R. 152

910. *PR. M. PR. Chettiar* v *Muniyandi Servai* 10 Rangoon 257
911. *Public Trustee* v *Letchumanan Chettiar* (1937) 2 Ceylon Law Journal 195
912. *R. M. N. L. Letchumanan Chettiar* v *A. L. V. Alagappa Chettiar* (1934) S. S. L. R. 114 (C.A.): also (1934) M.L.J. 50
913. *Ra. Ma. Pa. A. Sevugen Chetty* v *Ka. Ra. Chu. Colappan Chetty* (1863–68) Ramanathan Rep 209
914. *Ramanathan Chettiar* v *Marikar* (1929) 30 N. L. R. 234
915. *Ramanathan Chetty* v *Don Carolis* (1917) 19 N.L.R. 379
916. *Ramanathan Chetty* v *Jayasinghe* (1948) 50 N.L.R. 546
917. *Ramanathan Chetty* v *Meera Saibo Marikar* (1930) 32 N.L.R. 193
918. *Ramanathan Chetty* v *Mohideen* (1926) 8 Ceylon Law Recorder 42
919. *Ramanathan Chetty* v *Natchiya* (1923) 25 N.L.R. 83
920. *Ramanathan Chetty* v *Subramaniam Chetty* 28 I.C. 688
921. *Raman Chetti* v *Veerappa Chetti* 12 P.L.R. 126
922. *Raman Chettiar* v *Raman Chettiar* 14 P.L.R. 159
923. *Raman Chettiar* v *Vairavan Chettiar* (1942) 43 N.L.R. 183
924. *Raman Chettiar* v *Virappa* 13 P.L.R. 126
925. *Raman Chetty* v *George Steuart & Co.* (1884) 6 S.C.C. 159
926. *Raman Chetty* v *Mackwoods Ltd.* (1922) 24 N.L.R. 73
927. *Raman Chetty* v *Punchiappuhami* (1937) 40 N.L.R. 118
928. *Raman Chetty* v *Shawe* (1931) 33 N.L.R. 16
929 *Raman Chetty* v *Vyraven Chetty* (1916) 2 Ceylon Weekly Reporter 81
930. *Raman Chetty* v *Vyraven Chettiar* (1940) 41 N.L.R. 371
931. *Raman Chetty* v *Weerapatiren Kangany* (1910) 13 N.L.R. 331 (F.B.)
932. *Raman Chetty* v *Whittall* (1884) 6 S.C.C. 115
933. *Ramaswami Chettiar* v *Alagappa Chettiar* 28 M.L.J. 199
934. *Ramaswamy* v *Chetty* (1914) 18 N.L.R. 129
935. *Ramaswamy Chettiar* v *The Attorney General* (1936) 38 N.L.R. 313
936. *Rampershed Jewarry* v *Scheachurn Doss* 10 Moore's Indian Appeals 490
937. *Sadanathan* v *R. M. A. R. A. R. R. M. Arunachalam Chettiar* (1938) 2 Ceylon Law Journal 256

938. *Sathappa Chettiar* v *Song Chwee Oon* (1939) M.L.J. 180
939. *Savundranayagam* v *Savundranayagam* (1917) 20 N.L.R. 274
940. *Sawenna Weerappa Chetty* v *Kawenna Ana Alagappa Chetty* (1883) 6 S.C.C. 119
941. *Second Income-Tax Officer, City Circle VI, Madras and others* v *MCT. Trust and others* The Income-Tax Reports (Madras) Vol. 102. Part 4. 26 January 1976
942. *Segappa Chetty* v *Murugan Kamgany* (1897) 2 N.L.R. 375
943. *Sevugan Chetty* v *Colappan Chetty* (1863–68) Ramanathan Reports 209
944. *Sheik* v *Muhammad* I.L.R. 39 Madras 664 (at 669)
945. *Shellumbrum Chetty* v *Phillip Jones* 1 Ky. 204
946. *Shokalingam Chetty* v *Mrs. Ludovici* (1884) 6 S.C.C. 125
947. *Sidamparam Chetty* v *Jayasundera* (1914) 18 N.L.R. 171
948. *Sinnaiya Chetty* v *Solomons* (1885) 7 S.C.C. 104
949. *Sinnaiyah Chetty* v *Guy* (1881) 5 S.C.C. 40
950. *Siripina* v *Somasundaram Chetty* (1936) 38 N.L.R. 83
951. *Sithambaram Chettiar* v *Palaniappa Chettiar* (1902) 5 N.L.R. 353
952. *Sithambaram Chetty* v *Kelani Valley Rubber Co. Ltd.* (1922) 24 N.L.R. 163
953. *Sockalingam Chettiar* v *Gunawardena* (1909) 1 Current Law Reports 18
954. *Sockalingam Chettiar* v *Karuppan Chettiar* (1965) 68 N.L.R. 169
955. *Sockalingam Chettiar* v *Palaniappa Chettiar* (1934) S.S.L.R. 269; (1934) M.L.J. 207
956 *Sockalingam Chetty* v *Mohamadu Cassim* (1910) 2 Current Law Reports 18
957. *Somasunderam Chetti* v *Arunasalam Chetti* (1914) 17 N.L.R. 257
958. *Somasunderam Chetti* v *Todd* (1910) 13 N.L.R. 36
959. *Soundara Achi* v *Kalyani Achi & Ors.* (1953) M.L.J. 147, 149
960. *Subbaraya Pillai* v *Chidambaram Chettiar* 5 P.L.R. 176
961. *Subramaniam Chetty* v *S. A. S. Chellappa Chetty* (1918) M.W.N. 564
962. *Subramanian Chetty* v *Naidu* (1924) 26 N.L.R. 467
963. *Supperamaniam Chetty* v *Kanu Wappa* (1915) 1 Ceylon Weekly Report 155
964. *Supperamanian Chetty* v *Sophia* (1843–53) Ramanathan Reports 31

965. *Suppramaniam Chetty* v *Cave & Co* (1930) 32 N.L.R. 25
966. *Suppramaniam Chetty* v *Fiscal Western Province* (1916) 19 N.L.R. 129
967. *Suppramaniam Chetty* v *Katheru Ussen* (1884) 6 S.C.C. 71
968. *Suppramaniam Chetty* v *Mohamed Bhai* (1926) 27 N.L.R. 425
969. *Suppramaniam Chetty* v *Palaniappa Chetty* (1904) 3 Balasingham Reports 57
970. *Suppramaniam Chetty* v *White* (1908) 6 N.L.R. 182
971. *Swaminathan Chetty* v *Gordon Douglas* (1929) 32 N.L.R. 293
972. *Tan Kok Seng* v *Letchman Chetty* 1 Ky. 162
973. *Tharmalingam Chetty* v *Arunasalam Chettiar* (1944) 45 N.L.R. 414
974. *Tikam* v *Sundaram* (1933) A.I.R. Pat. 263
975. *Tillainathan* v *Ramasamy Chetty* (1900) 4 N.L.R. 328
976. *Toussaint* v *Somasunderam Chetty* (1920) 8 Ceylon Weekly Reporter 121
977. *Tyagaraja* v *Letchiman Chetty* (1926) 4 Times Law Reports 80
978. *Valliappa Chetty* v *Kamatchipillai* (1920) Ceylon Weekly Reporter 257
979. *Valliappa Chetty* v *Subbiah Pillai* (1938) 10 Ceylon Law Weekly 149
980. *Van Houten* v *Letchemanan Chetty* (1891) Tambiah Reports 49
981. *Velagappa Chettiar* v *Unnamalai Achi* (1917) N.W.N. 858
982. *Vellaiyappa Chetty* v *Nataraja* (1931) 58 I.A. 402: A. I. R. P.C. 294
983. *Vellayan Chetty* v *Duke* (1882) 5 S.C.C. 108
984. *Vellayappa Chettiar* v *Unnamalai Achi* 6 L.W. 687
985. *Venaithirthan Chetty* v *Appusamy* (1889) 6 S.C.C. 105
986. *Vengadasalam Chettiar* v *Ana Fernando* (1936) 38 N.L.R. 92
987. *Venkatachalam Chetty* v *Ramanathan Chetty* (1920) 39 Mad. L.J. 269
988. *Venkataraman* v *Janakai* (1939) 1 Mad. L.J. 520
989. *Vyraven Chettiar* v *Segappai Achy* (1940) 41 N.L.R. 398
990. *Vyravan Chetty* v *Ukku Benda* (1929) 27 N.L.R. 118
991. *Wass* v *Samaranayake* (1916) 19 N.L.R. 25 (N.B.)
992. *Wairavan Chetty* v *Jessan Saibo* (1906) 10 N.L.R. 118
993. *Wallayappa Chetty* v *Suppermaniam Chetty* (1881) 4 S.C.C. 91
994. *Wilson* v *Vijayalakshmi* (1931) 33 N.L.R. 260

## 12. NAGARATHARS IN SOUTH-EAST ASIA

995. Andrus, J.R., *Basic Problems of Relief, Rehabilitation and Reconstruction in South-East Asia* (Bombay: Oxford University Press, 1946)

996. Balbour, Surgen General Edward, *The Encyclopaedia of Asia and of Eastern and Southern Asia* See 8

997. Ball, W.M., *Nationalism and Communism in East Asia* (Melbourne: Melbourne University Press, 1956)

998. Cady, John F., *South East Asia: Its Historical Development* See 198

999. Callis, Helmut G., *Foreign Capital in South-East Asia* See 316

1000. Dobby, Ernest Henry George, *South-East Asia* (New York: John Wiley, 1951)

1001. Embree, John F. and Lillian O. Dotson, *Bibliography of the Peoples and Cultures of Mainland South-East Asia* See 575

1002. Evers, Hans Dieter, 'Chettiar Moneylender in South-East Asia See 341

1003. Furnivall, J. S., *Progress and Welfare in South-East Asia* (New York: Institute of Pacific Relations, 1941)

1004. ———, 'South Asia in the World Today' in Phillips Talbot (ed.), *South Asia in the World Today* (Chicago: University of Chicago Press, 1949)

1005. Hall, D. G. E., *A History of South-East Asia* See 210

1006. Harrison, B., *South-East Asia: A Short History* See 211

1007. Jacoby, E. H., *Agrarian Unrest in South-East Asia* See 374

1008. Karnow, Stanley and the Editors of LIFE, *South-East Asia* (New York: Times-Life Books, 1967)

1009. Le May, R., *The Culture of South-East Asia* See 579

1010. Mackenzie, Sir Compton, *Realms of Silver: One Hundred Years of Banking in the East* See 396

1011. Majumdar, R.C. *Ancient Indian Colonisation in South-East Asia* (Baroda: Oriental Institute, 1955)

1012. *Mobilization of Domestic Capital in Certain Countries of Asia and the Far East* See 407

1013. Mookerji, Radhakumud, 'Indian and Chinese Labour in the Agriculture of South-East Asia' See 409

1014. Mookerji, Sudhansu Bimal, ' Indian Minority in South-East Asia ' *Modern Review* (Calcutta) Vol. CXI. No. 2. 1962
1015. Nadarajan, M., ' The Nattukkottai Chettiar Community and South-East Asia ' See 274
1016. A Note on ' Indians Overseas—Indians in Indo-China ' *The Indian Review* (Madras) Vol. XLI. No. 11. November 1940
1017. Pillai, P. P. (ed.), *Labour in South-East Asia, a Symposium* See 431
1018. Pryor, Robin, J., *Bibliography on Internal Migration in South-East Asia* See 176
1019. Report of Seminars and Lectures, ' Chettiars and Hinduism in South-East Asia ' See 547
1020. Rose, Saul, *Socialism in South Asia* See 98
1021. Sastri, K. A. Nilakanta, *Some South Indian Influences in the Far East* (Bombay: Hind Kitabs, 1949)
1022. Scott, James C., *The Rural Economy of the Peasant Rebellion and Subsistence in South-East Asia* See 487
1023. Somalay, ' Chettiars and Hinduism in South-East Asia ' See 552
1024. Sovani, N. V., *Economic Relations of India with South-East Asia and the Far East* See 500
1025. Spencer, Robert, (ed.), *Religion and Change in Contemporary Asia* See 554
1026. Thompson, Virginia, ' Nationalism and Nationalist Movements in South-East Asia ' in R. Emerson, L. Mills, and V. Thompson (eds.), *Government and Nationalism in South-East Asia* Part III (New York: Institute of Pacific Relations, 1942)
1027. ———, *Labour Problems in South-East Asia* See 507
1028. Thompson, V. M. and R. Adloff, *Minority Problems in South-East Asia* (Stanford: Stanford University Press, 1955)
1029. Tinker, Hugh, *South Asia: A Short History* See 236
1030. Walter, F. Vella (ed.) *The Indianized States of South-East Asia by G. Coedes* (Kuala Lumpur: University of Malaya Press, 1967)
1031. Wickizer, V. D. and M. K. Bennett, *The Rice Economy of Monsoon Asia* (Stanford: Food Research Institute, 1941)

## 13. NAGARATHARS IN BURMA

1032. Adas, Michael, *The Burma Delta: Economic Development and Social Change on an Asian Rice Frontier, 1852–1941* See 291

1033. ———, 'Immigrant Asians and the Economic Impact of European Imperialism: The Role of the South Indian Chettiars in British Burma' See 292

1034. Ady, Peter, 'Economic Bases of Unrest in Burma' See 293

1035. *Agreement on Trade Between Burma and India*, 1941 (Rangoon: Government Press, 1941)

1036. *Agreement on Immigration between Burma and India*, 1941 (Rangoon: Government Press, 1941)

1037. Andrew, E.J.L., *Indian Labour in Rangoon* See 297

1038. Andrus J. R., *Rural Reconstruction in Burma* See 298

1039. ———, 'Three Economic Systems Clash in Burma' See 283

1040. ———, 'Foreign Investments in Burma' See 300

1041. ———, 'The Agrarian Problem in Burma' See 301

1042. ———, *Burmese Economic Life* See 302

1043. *Annual Administration Reports of the Government of Burma* 1900–36 (Rangoon: Government Press, 1900–1936)

1044. *Annual Season and Crop Reports of Burma* 1929–40 See 304

1045. Aung, Htin, 'Customary Law in Burma' in Phillip Thayer (ed.), *South East Asia in the Coming World* (Baltimore: The John Hopkins Press, 1953)

1046. ———, *Burmese Law Tales* (London: Oxford University Press, 1962)

1047. Banerjee, Anil Chandra, *Annexation of Burma* (Calcutta: A. Mukherjee and Bros., 1944)

1048. ———, *The Eastern Frontier of British India, 1784–1826* (Calcutta: A. Mukherjee and Bros., 1946)

1049. *Banking Enquiry Committee's Report* 1930 See 310

1050. Baxter, James, *Report on Indian Immigration* (Rangoon: Superintendent, Government Printing, 1941)

1051. Bennison, J. J., *Report of an Enquiry into the Standard of Living of the Working Classes in Rangoon* See 313

1052. Binns, B. O. *Agricultural Economy in Burma* See 315

1053. *The British Burma Gazetteer* (Rangoon: Superintendent Goverument Printing, 1880) 2 Vols
1054. Brown, R. Grant, 'The Origin of the Burmese' *Journal of the Burma Research Society* See 197
1055. ———, *Burma As I Saw It, 1889–1917* (London: Methuen, 1926)
1056. *Burma Gazetteers 1911* Vol. B *Akyab* (Rangoon: Superintendent, Government Printing, 1912, 1913)
1057. ———Vol. B *Amherst* (Rangoon: Superintendent, Government Printing, 1912, 1913)
1058. ———Vol. B *Bassein* (Rangoon: Superintendent, Government Printing, 1912, 13)
1059. ———Vol. B *Bhamo* (Rangoon: Superintendent, Government Printing, 1912, 1913)
1060. ———Vol. B *Hanthawaddy* (Rangoon: Superintendent, Government Printing, 1912, 1913)
1061. ———Vol. B *Henzada* (Rangoon: Superintendent, Government Printing, 1912, 1913)
1062. ———Vol. B *Hill District of Arakon* (Rangoon: Superintendent, Government Printing, 1912, 1913)
1063. ———Vol. B *Katha* (Rangoon: Superintendent, Government Printing, 1912, 1913)
1064. ———Vol. B *Kyaukpyu* (Rangoon: Superintendent, Government Printing, 1912, 1913
1065. ———Vol. B *Kyaukse* (Rangoon: Superintendent, Government Printing, 1912, 1913)
1066. ———Vol. B *Lower Chindwin* (Rangoon: Superintendent, Government Printing, 1912, 1913)
1067. ——— Vol. B *Magwe* (Rangoon: Superintendent, Government Printing, 1912, 1913)
1068. ———Vol. B *Mandalay* (Rangoon: Superintendent, Government printing, 1912, 1913)
1069. ———Vol. B *Ma-ubin* (Rangoon: Superintendent, Government Printing, 1912, 1913)
1070. ———Vol. B *Meiktila* (Rangoon: Superintendent, Government Printing, 1912, 1913)
1071. ———Vol. B *Merqui* (Rangoon: Superintendent, Government Printing, 1912, 1913)

1072. ———Vol. B *Minbu* (Rangoon: Superintendent, Government Printing, 1912, 1913)
1073. ———Vol. B *Myaungmya* (Rangoon: Superintendent, Government Printing, 1912, 1913)
1074. ———Vol. B *Myingyin* (Rangoon: Superintendent, Government Printing, 1912, 1913)
1075. ———Vol. B *Mytikyina* (Rangoon: Superintendent, Government Printing, 1912, 1913)
1076. ———Vol. B *Pakokku* (Rangoon: Superintendent, Government Printing, 1912, 1913)
1077. ———Vol. B *Pegu* (Rangoon: Superintendent, Government Printing, 1912, 1913)
1078. ———Vol. B *Prome* (Rangoon: Superintendent, Government Printing, 1912, 1913)
1079. ———Vol. B *Pyapon* (Rangoon: Superintendent, Government Printing, 1912, 1913)
1080. ———Vol. B *Ruby Mines* (Rangoon: Superintendent, Government Printing, 1912, 1913)
1081. ———Vol. B *Saging* (Rangoon: Superintendent, Government Printing, 1912, 1913)
1082. ———Vol. B *Salween* (Rangoon: Superintendent, Government Printing, 1912, 1913)
1083. ———Vol. B *Sandoway* (Rangoon: Superintendent, Government Printing, 1912, 1913)
1084. ———Vol. B *Shwebo* (Rangoon: Superintendent, Government Printing, 1912, 1913)
1085. ———Vol. B *Tavoy* (Rangoon: Superintendent, Government Printing, 1912, 1913)
1086. ———Vol. B *Tharawaddy* (Rangoon: Superintendent, Government Printing, 1912, 1913)
1087. ———Vol. B *Thaton* (Rangoon: Superintendent, Government Printing, 1912, 1913)
1088. ———Vol. B *Thayetmyo* (Rangoon: Superintendent, Government Printing, 1912, 1913)
1089. ———Vol. B *Toungoo* (Rangoon: Superintendent, Government Printing, 1912, 1913)
1090. ———Vol. B *Upper Chindwin* (Rangoon: Superintendent, Government Printing, 1912, 1913)

1091. ——Vol. B *Yamethin* (Rangoon: Superintendent, Government Printing, 1912, 1913)

1092. *Burma Rice* (Calcutta: Longmans, 1944)

1093. Butler, Sir Spencer Harcourt, *Speeches, 1923–1927* (Rangoon: Government Press, 1928)

1094. ——, 'Burma and its Problems' *Foreign Affairs* (New York) 1932

1095. Cady, F. John, 'Burma' in Lennox Mills (ed.), *The New World of South-East Asia* (Minneapolis: University of Minnesota Press, 1949)

1096. ——, 'Religion and Politics in Modern Burma' See 525

1097. ——, *A History of Modern Burma* (Ithaca, New York: Cornell University Press, 1958)

1098. Census of India 1891, Burma, *Report* Imperial Series Vol. I (Rangoon: Superintendent, Government Printing, 1892)

1099. Census of India 1901, Burma, *Report* Part I. Vol. XII (Rangoon: Superintendent, Government Printing, 1902)

1100. Census of India 1911, Burma, *Report* Part I. Vol. IX (India: Government Press, 1912)

1101. Census of India 1911, Burma, *Report* Part I, Vol. X (Rangoon: Superintendent, Government Printing, 1912)

1102. Census of India 1921, Burma, *Report* Part I, Vol. X (Rangoong Superintendent, Government Printing, 1922)

1103. Census of India 1931, Burma, *Report* Part I, Vol. XI. (India: Government Press, 1932)

1104. Census of India 1931, Burma, *Report* Part I, Vol. XII (Rangoon: Superintendent, Government Printing, 1932)

1105. Census of Burma (Incomplete) 1941, *Figures of Population* See 133

1106. Certain Conservative Members of Parliament, *A Blue-Print for Burma* (Bombay: Times of India Press, 1944)

1107. Chakkravarti, Nalini Ranjan, *The Indian Minority in Burma: The Rise and Decline of an Immigrant Community* See 201

1108. ——, *The Indian Minority in Burma* (London: Oxford University Press, 1971)

1109. Christian, John Leroy, *Modern Burma: A Survey of Political and Economic Development* See 327

1110. ———, *Burma and the Japanese Invader* (Bombay: Thacker, 1945) Revised Version of *Modern Burma*
1111. ———, *Burma* (London: Collins, 1945)
1112. ———, *Into Hidden Burma* (London: Faber and Faber, 1953)
1113. Clayton, H., *Rural Development in Burma* See 328
1114. Collis, M., *Trials in Burma* (London: Faber and Faber, 1955)
1115. ———, *Last and First in Burma* (London: Faber and Faber, 1955)
1116. *Constitution: Government of India Act, 1919 as extended to Burma* (*in Burma Legislative Council Manual* 1925) (Rangoon: Government Press, 1922)
1117. *Constitution of the Union of Burma* (Rangoon: Government Press, 1947)
1118. Cooper, Chester L., 'Money Lenders and the Economic Development of Lower Burma: An Exploratory Historical Study of the Role of Indian Chettiars' See 331
1119. Craddock, Sir Reginald, *Speeches, 1917–1922* (Rangoon: Government Press, 1924)
1120. ———, 'India and Burma: Some Contrasts' *The Asiatic Review* (London) Vol. XXI. January 1925
1121. Crosthwaite, Sir Charles, *The Pacification of Burma* (London: Edward Arnold, 1912)
1122. Darling, M. L., *Note on the Co-operative Movement in Burma* See 333
1123. Dautremer, Joseph, *Burma Uunder British Rule* Translated and with an introduction by Sir George Scott (London: T. Fisher Unwin, 1913)
1124. *Debates, Burma Legislative Council Rangoon* 1923–36 (Rangoon: Government Press, 1923–1936)
1125. *Debates, All-India (including Burma) Legislative Assembly* 1922–36 (New Delhi: Government Press, 1936)
1126. *Debates, Indian Legislative Assembly* 1937–42 (New Delhi: Government Press, 1937–42)
1127. *Debates, House of Lords* 1917–42 (London: His Majesty's Stationery Office, 1917–1942)
1128. *Debates, House of Commons 1917–42* (London: His Majesty's Stationery Office, 1917–1942)

1129. Desai, W. S., *History of the British Residency in Burma* (Rangoon: University of Rangoon: 1939)

1130. ———, *India and Burma* (Calcutta: Orient Longmans, 1954)

1131. De Terra, Helmut. ' Component Geography Factors of the Natural Regions of Burma ' *Annals of the Association of American Geographers* (Washington, D.C.) Vol. XXXIV June 1944

1132. *Divisional Reports on the Working of the Indian Factories Act in Lower Burma* See 336

1133. Donnison, F. S. V., *Public Administration in Burma: A Study of Development During the British Connexion* See 321

1134. D.C., (Probably Duroiselle Charles) ' A Handbook of Indian Companies Acts ' See 339

1135. Economic Planning Board, Government of Burma, *Two-Year Plan* See 340

1136. Enriques, C. M., *A Burmese Wonderland* (Calcutta: Thacker, 1922)

1137. Ferrars, Max and Bertha, *Burma* (London: Sampson, Low, Marston and Co., 1901)

1138. *Final Report of the Riot Enquiry Committee* (Rangoon: Superintendent, Government Printing, 1939)

1139. *First Annual Report on the Progress made giving effect to those Recommendations of the Royal Commission of Agriculture in India, 1928 which concern Burma* See 343

1140. *Fiscal and Economic Annual of Burma* See 445

1141. Forbes, C.J.F.S., *British Burma and Its People* (London: John Murray, 1878)

1142. Foreign Policy Association, ' Burma, An Experiment in Self-Government ' *Foreign Policy Report* (New York: 1945)

1143. Furnivall, J. S., *Report of the First Regular Settlement Operations in the Myingyan District, Season*1909–1911 Burma Settlement Department (Rangoon: Superintendent, Government Printing, 1912)

1144. ———, *An Introduction to the Political Economy of Burma* See 347

1145. ———, *The Beginnings of British Rule in Burma* (Rangoon: Burma Research Society, 1939)

1146. ———, ' The Fashioning of Leviathan ' *Journal of the Burma Research Society* (Rangoon) Vol. XXIX. 1939

1147. ———, 'Burma, Past and Present' *Far Eastern Survey* (New York) 25 February 1953

1148. ———, *Colonial Policy and Practice: A Comparative Study of Burma and Netherlands India* (New York: New York University Press, 1956)

1149. ———, *The Governance of Modern Burma* (New York: Institute of Pacific Relations, 1958)

1150. Furnivall, J. S., and R. Morrison, *Burma Gazetteer, Insein District* Vol. A (Rangoon: Superintendent, Government Printing, 1914)

1151. Geary, Grattan, *Burma After the Conquest, Viewed in Its Political, Social and Commercial Aspects from Mandalay* See 258

1152. *Government Anniversary Reports* (Rangoon: Superintendent, Government Printing, 1950–1958)

1153. Government of Burma, *Notes and Statistics* (Rangoon: Superintendent, Government Printing, 1890)

1154. ———, *A Handbook of Agriculture for Burma* See 350

1155. ———, *Agriculture in Burma* See 351

1156. ———, *Agricultural Leaflets* See 352

1157. ———, *The Marketing Crops in Burma* See 353

1158. ———, *List of Industrial Establishments in Burma*, 1929 See 354

1159. ———, *List of Industrial Establishments in Burma* 1933 See 355

1160. ———, *List of Industrial Establishments in Burma* 1936 See 356

1161. ———, *Trade in Agricultural Products* See 357

1162. ———, *Report on the Working of Co-operative Societies in Burma for the Year Ending June* 30, 1940 See 480

1163. ———, *Burma Handbook* (Simla: Government of Burma, 1941)

1164. ———, *Burma Handbook* (Simla: Government of Burma, 1943)

1165. ———, *Burma Handbook* (Simla: Superintendent, Government Printing, 1944)

1166. ———, *Economic Survey of Burma* See 358

1167. Grant, W. J., *The New Burma* (London: George Allen and Unwin, 1940)

1168. ———, *The Rice Crop in Burma: Its History, Cultivation, Marketing and Improvement* See 359

1169. Gupta, Sisir, *India and Regional Integration in Asia* See 39

1170. Hagen, Everitt Einer, *The Economic Development of Burma* See 363

1171. Hall, D. G. E., *Early English Intercourses with Burma* (1587–1743) (London: Longmans, 1928)

1172. ———, *Europe and Burma* (London: Oxford University Press, 1945)

1173. ———, *Burma* (London: Hutchinson's University Library, 1950)

1174. Hanks, L. M. Jr. ' The Quest for Individual Autonomy in the Burmese Personality with particular Reference to the Arakan ' *Psychiatry* (Washington D.C.) Vol. XII. 1949

1175. Harvey G. E., *History of Burma* See 212

1176. ———, ' Burma, 1782–1852 ' in H. H. Dodwell, (ed.) *The Cambridge History of India* See 213

1177. ———, ' The Conquest of Upper Burma ' in H. H. Dodwell (ed.) *The Cambridge History of the British Empire* (Cambridge: Cambridge University Press, 1932) Vol. V. (This volume is the same as Vol. VI of *The Cambridge History of India*)

1178. ———, *The British Rule in Burma 1824–1942* (London: Faber and Faber, 1945)

1179. Hobbs, C., ' Nationalism in British Colonial Burma ' *Far Eastern Quarterly* (U.S.A.) February 1947

1180. Huke, Robert E., ' Rice in Burma: A Geographic Analysis of Three Agricultural Villages ' See 366

1181. Indian Statutory Commission. *Memorandum submitted by the Government of Burma* (London: His Majesty's Stationery Office, 1930)

1182. *Indo-Burma Immigration Agreement All Party Protest* (Madras, 1941)

1183. *The Indo-Burma Immigration Agreement A Nation in Protest* (New Delhi, 1941)

1184. Information Department, Burma Office. *Burma: Policy of His Majesty's Government*, 1945 (Statements of Policy and official Speeches, 1945) (London, February 1946)

1185. *Interim Report of the Riot Enquiry Committee* (Rangoon: Superintendent, Government Printing, 1939)

1186. *Interim Report of the Committee Appointed to Enquire into the Rice and Paddy Trade* See 370

1187. Ireland, Alleyne, *The Province of Burma* (Boston: Houghton, Mifflin, 1907) 2 Volumes

1188. Isaac, P. M. 'Burma Government's Land Purchase Scheme' See 123

1189. Johnston, William, C., *Burma's Foreign Policy* (Cambridge, Mass: M.I.T. Press, 1965)

1190. Kelly, R. Talbot, *Burma, The Land and the People* See 124

1191. Knappen, Tippetts, Abett and McCarthy, *Comprehensive Report: Economic and Engineering Development prepared for the Government of the union of Burma* See 385

1192. Kozicki, Richard J., 'India and Burma, 19371–957: A Study in International Relations' Unpublished doctoral dissertation, University of Pennsylvania, Philadelphia, 1959

1193. Kyaw Min, U., *The Burma We Love* (Calcutta: Bharati Bhavan, 1945)

1194. Lahiri, Sisir Chandra, *Principles of Modern Burmese Buddhist Law* See 536

1195. Leach, F. Burton, *The Future of Burma* (Rangoon: British Burma Press, 1936)

1196. ———, 'The Rice Industry of Burma' See 390

1197. *The Lower Burma Land Revenue Manual* (*Containing the Lower Burma Land and Revenue Act of* 1876) See 394

1198. Luce, G. H., 'Burma's Debt to pagan' *Journal of the Burma Research Society* (Rangoon) Vol. XXII. 1932

1199. Mahajani, Usha, *The Role of Indian Minorities in Burma and Malaya* (Bombay: Vora, 1960)

1200. Malcom, Howard, *Travels in the Burman Empire* (Edinburgh: William and Robert Chambes, 1840)

1201. Masters, Allene, 'The Chettiars in Burma: An Economic Survey of a Migrant Community' See 402

1202. Maung, Maung, *Burma in the Family of Nations* (Amsterdam: Djambaton, 1956)

1203. ———, *Burm a'sConstitution* (The Hague: Martinus Nihjoff, 1959)

1204. Maurice, Collis, *The Burmese Scene: Political-Historical-Pictorial* See 189

1205. *Memorandum of the Government of Burma to the Indian Statutory Commission* (*Simon Commission*) 1928–29 (Rangoon: Government Press, 1928–1929)

1206. *Memorandum of Financial Settlement between Burma and India* See 405

1207. *Memorandum* (*unsigned, typewritten*) *from an Official of the Government of Burma, Labelled 'Confidential' and dated July* 27, 1932 in Darwood Collection of Manuscripts, Anes Library of South-East Asia, University of Minnesota, Minneapolis

1208. Mi Mi, Khaing, *Burmese Family* (Calcutta: Longmans. 1940).

1209. Ministry of Agriculture and Forests. *The Land Nationalisation Act 1948* (Rangoon: Superintendent, Government Printing, 1950)

1210. ———, 'Speech Delivered by the Hon'ble Thakin Nu, Prime Minister in Support of Land Nationalisation Bill' Printed with *The Land Nationalisation Act 1948* (Rangoon: Superintendent, Government Printing, 1950)

1211. Morris, A. P., *Report on the Development of Industries in Burma* See 411

1212. Moscotti, Albert D., 'British Policy in Burma, 1917–1937: A Study in the Development of Colonial Self-Rule' Un-Published Ph. D. dissertation, Yale University, New Haven, 1950

1213. Nagarajan, K., 'The Road to Mandalay' in B. V. N. Naidu (ed.) *Rajah Sir Annamalai Chettiar Commemoration Volume* (Annamalai Nagar: Annamalai University, 1941)

1214. Nisbet, John, *Burma under British Rule And Before* (Westminster: Archibald Constable and Co., 1901) 2 Volumes

1215. Noel-Paton, Frederick, *Burma Rice* See 417

1216. A Note on 'The Madras Legislative Council — Safeguards for Indians in Burma' *The Indian Annual Register* (Calcutta) Vol. II. No. 14. July-December 1931

1217. A Note on 'The Burma Legislative Council—Budget Session-Rangoon' *The Indian Annual Register* (Calcutta) Vol. 1. No. 16. January-June 1933

1218. A Note on 'Proceedings and Resolutions Separation of Burma' *The Indian Annual Register* (Calcutta) Vol. 1. No. 18. January-June 1935

1219. A Note on 'The Burma Legislative Council—Rangoon-Madras Mail Service' *The Indian Annual Register* (Calcutta) Vol. I. No. 19. January-June 1936.

1220. A Note on 'Indians Overseas—Burma—Remittances from Burma' *The Indian Review* (Madras) Vol. 50. No. 11. November 1949

1221. A Note on 'Indians Outside India—Burma—Compensation for Indians' *The Indian Review* (Madras) Vol. 58. No. 4. April 1957

1222. A Note on 'Indians Outside India—Burma' *The Indian Review* (Madras) Vol. 59. No. 8. August 1958

1223. A Note on 'Indians Outside India—Burma' *The Indian Review* (Madras) Vol. 59. No. 9. September 1958

1224. A Note on 'Burma' *Modern Review* (Calcutta) Vol. CXI. No. 1. 1962

1225. A Note on 'Indian Interests in Burma' *Modern Review* (Calcutta) Vol. LXXXX. No. 3. 1951

1226. *Notes by the Indian Advisory Committee to the Burma Nattukkottai Chettiars' Association on the Land Nationalisation Act 1948* (Chettinad: K. E. S. C. Ltd., 1948)

1227. Odell, Francis David, *Market Surveys of Burma Crops* See 422

1228. *The Origin and Causes of the Burma Rebellion 1930–32* (Rangoon: Superintendent, Government Printing, 1934)

1229. Parker, H., 'The Rice Industry of Burma' See 427

1230. Pearn, B. R., 'The Commercial Treaty of 1862' See 428.

1231. ———, *A History of Rangoon* See 221

1232. ———, *The Indians in Burma: Racial Relations Studies in Conflict and Co-operation No.* 4 (Herefordshire, England: LePlay House Press, 1946)

1233. Phayre, Arthur P., *History of Burma* See 222

1234. *Proceedings—Burma Round Table Conference*, Cmd. 4004 (London: 1931–32)

1235. Pye, Lucian, W., *Politics, Personality and Nation Building: Burma's Search for Identity* (London: Yale University Press, 1962)

1236. Rafi, M. Mirza, *The Problems of Indian Settlers in Burma* (New Delhi: The Indian Institute of International Affairs, 1946)

1237. *Rangoon Gazettee* Rangoon, 12 August 1935

1238. *Rangoon Gazette* Rangoon, 5 July 1937
1239. *Rangoon Gazette* Rangoon, 18 June 1940
1240. Rao, A. Narayan, *Indian Labour in Burma* See 435
1241. Ray, Nihar-Ranjan, *Brahmanical Gods in Burma: A Chapter of Indian Art and Iconography* See 545
1242. ———, *Sanskrit Buddhism in Burma* See 546
1243. *Report on the Administration of the Province of Pegu 1855–1861* (Rangoon: Superintendent, Government Printing, 1856–62)
1244. *Report on the Administration of Tenasserim and Martaban Provinces* 1856–1861 (Rangoon: Superintendent, Government Printing, 1857–62)
1245. *Report on the Trade and Customs of Burma, 1867–1875* See 439
1246. *Report on the Census of British Burma*, 1872 (Rangoon: Superintendent, Government Printing, 1875)
1247. *Reports on the Trade and Navigation of Burma 1875–1902* See 442
1248. *Report on Settlement Operations in the Syrian Townships, Hanthawaddy Districts, Season 1879–80* (Rangoon: Superintendent, Government Printing, 1880)
1249. *Report on Settlement Operations in the Bassein District, Season* 1880–81 (Rangoon: Government Press, 1880)
1250. *Report on the Census of British Burma, 1881* (Rangoon: Superintendent, Government Printing, 1882)
1251. *Report of Maritime Trade and Customs 1881–82* (Rangoon: Superintendent, Government Printing, 1883)
1252. *Report on the Settlement Operations in the Hanthawaddy District, Season 1881–82* (Rangoon: Superintendent, Government Printing, 1882)
1253. *Report on the Settlement Operations in the Bassein District, Season* 1881–82 (Rangoon: Government Press, 1883)
1254. *Reports on the Revenue Administration of British Burma 1867–1935* See 440
1255. *Report on the Settlement Operations in the Bassein District, Season* 1882–83 (Rangoon: Government Press, 1884)
1256. *Report on the Settlement Operations in the Bassein and Henzada Districts, Season 1883–84* (Rangoon: Government Press, 1885)

1257. *Report on the Revision Settlement Operations in the Tharawaddy District, Season 1901–02* (Rangoon: British Burma Press, 1903)

1258. *Report on the Maritime Trade of Burma, 1902–1906* See 443

1259. *Report on the Administration of Burma for the Year 1906–1907* (Rangoon: Superintendent, Government Printing, 1907)

1260. *Report on the Settlement of the Paung, Pa-an and Hlainglwa Districts, Season 1908–1911* (Rangoon: Superintendent, Government Printing, 1912)

1261. *Report on the Second Settlement of Hyaunglebin Subdivision and Original Settlement of a Part of Thanatpin Township of the Pegu District, Season 1911–1913* (Rangoon: Superintendent, Government Printing, 1914)

1262. *Report of the Second Settlement of the Main Portion of the Nagaputaw Township and Third Settlement of the Southern Portion of the Bassein Township of the Bassein District, Season* 1912–1913 (Rangoon: Superintendent, Government Printing, 1914)

1263. *Report on the Administration of Burma, 1914–15* (Rangoon: Superintendent, Government Printing, 1915)

1264. *Report on the Land Revenue Administration of Burma During the Year Ending the* 30*th June* 1914 See 446

1265. *Report on the Third Settlement of the Kawa Township of the Pegu District, Season 1913–14* (Rangoon: Superintendent, Government Printing, 1915)

1266. *Report on the Settlement of the Kyaukpyu District, Season 1909–13* (Rangoon: Supeintendent, Government Printing, 1915)

1267. *Report on the First Regular Settlement in the Myinglyan District, Season 1903–13* (Rangoon: Superintendent, Government Printing, 1915)

1268. *Report of the Committee on Educational Reform in Burma* (Rangoon: Government Press, 1916)

1269. *Report on the Third Settlement of the Tharawaddy District, Season 1913–15* (Rangoon: British Burma Press, 1916)

1270. *Report on Settlement Operations Being Original Settlement in the Sinbaungive Township and in Parts of the Minbla, Thayetmyo and Allanmyo Township and Revision Settlement in Parts of the Thayetomyo, Allammyo and Mindon Townships of the Thayetmyo*

*District, Season 1913–16* (Rangoon: Superintendent, Government Printing, 1917)

1271. *Report on the Settlement of the Kyaukpya District, Season 1914–16* (Rangoon: Superintendent, Government Printing, 1918)
1272. *Report on the Administration of Burma for the Year 1918–19* (Rangoon: Superintendent, Government Printing, 1920)
1273. *Report of the Rangoon University Committee* (Rangoon: Government Press, 1920)
1274. *Report on the Administration of Burma for the Year 1920–21* (Rangoon: Superintendent, Government Printing, 1922)
1275. *Report of the Burma Reforms Committee* (Whyte Committee) (London: His Majesty's Stationery Office, 1922)
1276. *Report of the Committee on Burma Land Revenue System* (Furnivall Committee) See 448
1277. *Report on the Administration of Burma for the Year 1921–22* (Rangoon: Superintendent, Government Printing, 1923)
1278. *Report on the Administration of Burma for the year 1923–24* (Rangoon: Superintendent, Government Printing, 1925)
1279. *Report on the Conditions of Agricultural Tenants and Labour in Burma* (Couper Committee) See 449
1280. *Report on the Original Settlement of the Mamank Tract in the Kawa Township of the Pegu District, Season 1924–25* (Rangoon: Superintendent, Government Printing, 1926)
1281. *Report on the Administration of Burma for the Year 1926–27* (Rangoon: Superintendent, Government Printing, 1928)
1282. *Report of the Royal Commission on Agriculture in India* See 450
1283. *Report on the Standard and Cost of Living of the Working Classes in Rangoon* See 451
1284. *Report of the Committee on Co-operation in Burma, 1928–29* (Rangoon: Superintendent, Government Printing, 1929)
1285. *Report of the Agricultural Finance Committee* See 454
1286. *Report of the Provincial Banking Enquiry Committee 1929–30, Banking and Credit in Burma* See 455
1287. *Report of the Provincial Banking Enquiry Committee, Burma 1929–30* See 457
1288. *Report on the Settlement Operations in the Upper Chindwin District, Season 1926–28* (Rangoon: Superintendent, Government Printing, 1930)

1289. *Report on the Administration of Burma for the year 1929–1930* (Rangoon: Superintendent, Government Printing, 1930)

1290. *Report on the Rebellion in Burma upto 3rd May, 1931 and Communique issued by the Government of Burma,* 19*th May, 1931* Cmd. 3900 (London: His Majesty's Stationery Office, 1931)

1291. *Report on the Second Revision Settlement of the Kyaikto and Thaton Subdivisions of the Thaton District of Lower Burma, Season 1926–30* (Rangoon: Superintendent, Government Printing 1931)

1292. *Report on the Third Revision Settlement of the Hanthawaddy District 1930–33* (Rangoon: Superintendent, Government Printing, 1934)

1293. *Report on the Land Revenue Administration of Burma During the Year Ending* 30*th June 1934* See 462

1294. *Report on the Land Revenue Administration of Burma During the Year Ending* 30*th June 1935* See 463

1295. *Report on the Revision settlement of the Insein District Season 1933–35* (Rangoon: Superintendent, Government Printing, 1936)

1296. *Report on the Administration of Burma* (Rangoon: Superintendent Government Printing, 1931–1936)

1297. *Report on the Land Revenue Administration of Burma During the Year Ending* 30*th June 1936* See 464

1298. *Report on the Revision Settlement of the Pegu District Season 1932–34* (Rangoon: Superintendent, Government Printing, 1937)

1299. *Report of the Rice Export Trade Enquiry Committee* See 465

1300. *Report on the Land and Agriculture Committee-Tenancy* See 467

1301. *Report on the Land and Agriculture Committee—Land Alienation* See 468

1302. *Reports of the Burma Fiscal Committee, 1938–39* See 469

1303. *Reports on the Trade and Customs Administration of Burma 1906–1937* See 444

1304. *Reports on the Operations of the Department of Agriculture 1906–1940* See 445

1305. *Report of the Riot Enquiry Committee* (Rangoon: Government Press, 1938)

1306. *Reports on the Maritime Trade and Customs Administration of Burma 1906–1937* See 466

1307. *Report of the Burma Secretariat Incident Committee* (Rangoon: Government Press, 1939)

1308. *Reports on the Working of the Cooperative Societies Act in Burma, 1905–1940* See 470

1309. *Reports on the Working of the Indian Factories Act in Burma 1911–1940* See 471

1310. *Report on the Marketing of Rice in India and Burma* See 472

1311. *Reports of the Burma Land and Agricultural Committee 1938–40* (I-IV) See 473

1312. *Report on the Land and Agriculture Committee-Agricultural Finance, Colonization and Land Purchase* See 474

1313. *Report on the Land and Agricultural Committee-Regulation of Money lending and Agricultural Finance* See 475

1314. *Report on the Revision Settlement of the Nyaungmya District Season 1933–35* (Rangoon: Superintendent, Government Printing, 1939)

1315. *Reports on Public Instruction in Burma 1920–40* (Rangoon Government Press, 1920–1940)

1316. *Reports on Municipal Administration, City of Rangoon 1930–40* (Rangoon: Government Press, 1930–1940)

1317. *Report of the Committee on Expenditure on Public Services* See 477.

1318. *Reports of Police Administration, Burma 1900–41* (Rangoon: Government Press, 1900-1941)

1319. *Report of the Bribery and Corruption Enquiry Committee* (Rangoon: Home Department, Superintendent, Government Printing 1941)

1320. *Report on Indian Immigration—Burma* (Rangoon: Government Press, 1941)

1321. *Report on the Immigration of Indians into Burma* (Baxter Commission) (Rangoon: Government Press, 1941)

1322. *Report of the Burma Village Administration Committee* (Rangoon: Government Press, 1941)

1323. *Report of the University Enquiry Committee* (Rangoon: Government Press, 1941)

1324. *Report on the Revision Settlement of the Bassein District Together with the original Settlement of Certain Areas in the Yegyi, Thabaung, Bassein West and Ngaputaw Townships, Season 1935–39* (Rangoon: Superintendent, Government Printing, 1941)

1325. *Report on the Development of small-scale and Cottage Industries in Industries in Burma* See 481

1326. Reshick, Stephen A, *A Socio-economic Inter-relation of the Decline of Rural Industry under Export Expansion: A Comparison Among Burma, Philippines and Thailand 1870–1938* See 483

1327. Robertson, C. J., ' The Rice Export from Burma, Siam and French Indo-China ' See 484

1328. *Royal Commission of Agriculture in India and Burma* See 485

1329. Rutledge, G., ' Some Notes on the Burma Census ' *Journal of the Burma Research Society* (Rangoon) II (ii) December 1912

1330. *Scheme of Constitutional Reform in Burma if separated from India* Rangoon, 1933

1331. Scott, J. G., *Burma: A Handbook of Practical, Commercial and Political Information* See 488

1332. ———, *Burma: From the Earliest Times to the Present Day* See 231

1333. ———, (*Shway Yoe*) *The Burman, His Life and Notions* (London: Macmillan, 1927)

1334. *Season and Crop Report* See 489

1335. *Season and Crop Report* See 490

1336. Sein, Ma Mya, *Burma*, (London: Oxford University Press, 1944)

1337. Sen, Nirmal Chandra, *A Peep into Burma Politics 1917–1932* (Allahabad: Kitabistan, 1945)

1338. Siegelman, Phillip, ' Colonial Development and the Chettiar: A Study in Political-Economic Ecology of Modern Burma ' See 495

1339. Siok-Hwa, Cheng, *The Rice Industry of Burma 1852–1940* See 496

1340. Spate, O. H. K., ' The Burmese Village ' *Geographical Review* (New York) Vol. XXX. October 1945

1341. Stamp, L. Dudley, 'Burma—An Under Developed Monsoon Country' *Geographical Review* (New York) Vol. XXX January 1930

1342. ———, *A New Geography of India, Burma and Ceylon* See 108

1343. *Statements of the Sea-borne Trade and Navigation of Burma 1855-1940* See 501

1344. Stuart, J., 'Why Burma is Sparsely Peopled' See 184

1345. Thager, F., 'Burma—Land of Golden Pagodas' *Headline Series* (New York) March-April 1954

1346. Thein, Pe, *What Happened in Burma* (Allahabad: Kitabistan, 1948)

1347. Thompson, V., 'The New Nation of Burma' *Far-Eastern Survey* (New York) Vol. XVII. No. 7, 7 April 1948

1348. Tinker, Hugh, *The Foundations of Local Self-Government in India Pakistan and Burma* See 112

1349. ———, 'A Forgotten Long March: The Indian Exodus from Burma, 1942' *Journal of South -East Asian Studies* (Singapore) Vol. VI. No. 1, 1975

1350. ———, *The Union of Burma* (London: Oxford University Press, 1957)

1351. *Trade and Immigration Relations Between India and Burma After the Separation of Burma* See 508

1352. Trager, Frank N., 'Review of U Tun Wai: Burma's Currency and Credit' See 509

1353. ———, *Burma from Kingdom to Republic* See 237

1354. Frank N., John N. Musgrave and Janet Welsh, *Annotated Bibliography of Burma* (New Haven: Human Relations Area Files, 1956)

1355. Tun Wai, U., *Burma's Currency and Credit* See 510

1356. ———, *Economic Development of Burma from 1800* to *1940* See 511

1357. US Office of Strategic Services. *Japanese Administration of Burma* R and A No. 2015. Washington D.C. 1944

1358. Walinsky, L. J., *Economic Development in Burma 1951–60* See 415

1359. White, H. T., *A Civil Servant in Burma* (London: Edward Arnold, 1913)

1360. ———, *Burma* (Cambridge: Cambridge University Press, 1923)

1361. Wright. A., H. A. Cartwright and R. Breakspear (eds.), *Twentieth Century Impressions of Burma* (London: Llyod's Greater Britain Publishing Co., 1910)

1397. Goonatilake, H. A. I., *A Bibliography of Ceylon* 3 Volumes (Zug, Switerland: Inter-Documentation Company, 1970-1973)

1398. Gunasekara, H. A. de. S., *From Dependent Currency to Central Banking in Ceylon* See 362

1399. Gupta, Ajoy Kumar, The Ceylon Citizenship Question and the Indian Problem *The Modern Review* (Calcutta) Vol. 100. No. 1. July 1956

1400. Cave, Henry W., *Golden Tips—A Description of Ceylon and Its* Great Tea Industry (London: Simpson, Low and Marston, Co., 1900)

1401. Hulgalla, H. A. J., *Ceylon* (Ceylon: Ceylon Government Department, 1957)

1402. Idaikkadar, N. Manicka, ' Hindu Shrines of the Vanni ' See 535

1403. Indrapala, K., ' Some Medieval Mercantile Communities of South India and Ceylon ' See 368

1404. Jackson, Sir Edward, *Report of a Commission on Immigration into Ceylon*(Colombo: Ceylon Government Press, 1938)

1405. Jenkins, Richard Wade, *Ceylon in the Fifties and Eighties* (Colombo: A.M. and J. Ferguson, 1886)

1406. Karunatilake, J. N. S., *Banking and Financial Institutions in Ceylon* See 382

1407. Kodikara, S. U., *Indo-Ceylon Relations Since Independence* See 50

1408. Macmillan, Allister, *Seaports of India and Ceylon* See 55

1409. Marjoribanks, N. E., and A. K. G. Ahmad Thambi Marakkayar, *Report on Indian Labour Emigrating to Ceylon and Malaya* See 401

1410. Marshall, R. Singer, *The Emerging Elite: A Study of Political Leadership in Ceylon* (Cambridge: The MIT Press, 1969)

1411. *Memorandum Presented by Ccylon Indian Congress to the Immigration Commission*, Colombo, 1937

1412. *Memorandum of the Ceylon Indian Congress on the Joint Report of the Delegations from India and Ceylon*, Colombo, 25 October 1941

1413. Nattukottai Chettiars ' Association's Memorandum before the Ceylon Banking Commission See 416

1414. Nevill, Hugh, ' The Hittites in India ' *Taprobanian* (Colombo) August 1887

1415. ———, ' The Vanniars ' *The Taprobanian* (Colombo) 1887

1416. A Note on ' Indians Overseas—Ceylon Indian Congress ' *The Indian Review* (Madras) Vol. XLI. No. 10. October 1940

1417. A Note on ' Indians Outside India—Ceylon—Stateless Indians ' *The Indian Review* (Madras) Vol. 62. No. 5 May 1961

1418. Pillai, K. K., *South India and Ceylon* See 81

1419. Ragavan, M. D., *The Tamils in Ceylon: India in Ceylonese History, Society and Culture,* See 225

1420. Ramadas, R. V., India and Sri Lanka: Towards Amicable Settlement ' In R. V. Ramadas (ed.), *Indians in Sri Lanka* (Bombay: Purushotamadas Thakurudas Research Centre, 1977)

1421. *Report on Ceylon Census* 1901 Colombo Vol. 1. 1901

1422. *Report of the State Mortgage Bank* See 453

1423. *Report of the Ceylon Banking Commission—Memoranda and Evidence* See 460

1424. *Report of the Ceylon Banking Commission—Memorandum and Evidence* See 461

1425. *Report of the Sub-Committee Commercial Legislation* See 476

1426. *Report of the Select Committee of Relief to Debtors* See 459

1427. Shenoy, B. R., *Ceylon Currency and Banking* See 493

1428. Singer, Marshall R., *The Emerging Elite: A Study of Political Leadership in Ceylon* (Cambridge, Mass: The MIT Press, 1964)

1429. Sivaratnam, C., *An Outline of the Cultural History and Principles of Hinduism* See 551

1430. ———, *The Tamils in Early Ceylon* (Colombo: United Merchants Ltd., 1968)

1431. Skeen, George, *The Passenger's Guide to Colombo* (Colombo: A. M. and J. Ferguson, 1906)

1432. Stamp, Dudley L., *A New Geography of India, Burma and Ceylon* See 108

1433. Tambiah, H. W., *Laws and Customs of the Tamils of Ceylon* See 586

1455. Chai Hon-Chan, *The Development of British Malaya: 1896-1909* (Kuala Lumpur: Oxford University Press, 1964)

1456. Challis, Joyce, *Annotated Bibliography of Economic and Social Material: West Malaysia* See 320

1457. ———, *Annotated Bibliography of Economic and Social Material in Sabah and Sarawak* See 321

1458. ———, *Annotated Bibliography of Economic and Social Material Singapore and West Malaysia* See 322

1459. Chander, Ramesh, ' Malaysia: A Population Dossier ' See 161

1460. Chander, R. and J. M. N., *General Report: Population Census of Malaysia*, 1970, Vol. 2 (Kuala Lumpur: Department of *in* Statistics, 1975)

1461. ———, (eds.), *The Population of Malaysia* See 162

1462. Cheah Boon Kheng, ' Money-Lenders ' See 324

1463. Chettiar, O. R. MM. SP. SV. AN. Annamalai, ' Tamil Culture in Malaysia ' See 571

1464. Chettur, S. K., *Malayan Adventure* (Mangalore: Basel Mission Press, 1948)

1465. Clarence, E. Glick, ' Leaders of Indian Origin in Kuala Lumpur ' in Xavier S. Thaninayagam (ed.), *Proceedings of the First International Conference Seminar of Tamil Studies* (Kuala Lumpur: International Association of Tamil Research, 1969), Vol. 1

1466. ———, ' The Changing Positions of Two Tamil Groups in Western Malaya ' in R. E. Asher (ed.), *Proceedings of the Second International Conferencee—Seminar of Tamil Studies* (Madras: International Association of Tamil Research, 1971)

1467. Clearing House Service for Population Education. *Bibliography on Population Education, Malaysia* (Bangkok: UNESCO Regional Office for Education in Asia, 1976)

1468. Colaco, Lucy, ' Labour Emigration from India to the British Colonies of Ceylon, Malaya, and Fiji aduring the years 1850-1921 '. See 330

1469. Cole, Fay Cooper, *The Peoples of Malaysia* See 257

1470. Devahuti, D., *India and Ancient Malaya from the Earliest Times to Circa A. D. 1400* See 204

1471. Dey, Mukul K., ' The Ethnic Groups of Malaya: A Population Study ' See 167

1472. Federated Malay States. *Report and Proceedings of the Committee to Consider Why the System of Small Loans to Native Agriculturists had failed in Perak* See 342

1473. Fernandez Dorothy Z., ' Population Levels, Trends and Planning in Malaysia ' See 168

1474. Firth, Raymond, *Malay Fishermen: Their Peasant Economy* See 344

1475. *A Full Report of the Proceedings of a Meeting held on* 6-1-1924 *at the Marimaman Temple, High Street, Kuala Lumpur to Concert Measures for the good Government of the Temple and its Funds* See 534

1476. George, Netto, *Indians in Malaya: Historical Facts and Figures* See 219

1477. Ghosh, B. C., ' Comment And Criticism- Malayan Indian Congress ' *Modern Review* (Calcutta) Vol. LXXXIV. No. 4. 1948

1478. Ginsberg, N. S., and G. F. Robert, *Malaya* (Seattle: University of Washington Press, 1958)

1479. Govindaswamy, Palanivel, ' A Study of the Background to Malayan Indian Politics, 1900-1941 ' Thesis Submitted for The Degree of Bachelor of Arts, University of Malaya, Kuala Lump ur, 1972

1480. Gullick, J. M., *Malaysia* (London: Benn, 1969)

1481. Gungwu, Wang (ed.), *Malaysia: A Survey* (Singapore: Donald Moore Books, 1964)

1482. Hawkins, G., ' Reactions to the Malayan Union ' *Pacific Affairs* (New York) Setpember 1946

1483. Hawley, A. H., Dorothy Fernandes and Vasantha Kandiah, *The Expectation of Working Life in Peninsular Malaysia,* 1970 See 364

1484. Hirschman,Charles, *Estimates of the Inter-Censal Population* by *Sex, Community and Age Group, Peninsular Malaysia, 1957-1970* See 169

1485. ———, ' A Note on Past and future Trends in Population Growth in Malaysia ' See 170

1486. Hughes, David R., *The Peoples of Malaya* See 262

1487. *Input-Output Tables Peninsular Malaysia* 1970 (Kuala Lumpur: Department of Statistics, 1971)

1488. Institute of Race Relations, London, *Indians in Malaysia and Singapore* (Kuala Lumpur: Oxford University Press, 1970)

1489. Iyer, K. A. Neelanandha, *Indian Problem in Malaya* (Kuala Lumpur: Federated Malay States, The Indian Office, 1938)

1490. Jackson, James C., ' Population Changes in Selangor State, 1850–1891 ' See 171

1491. Kaur, Amarjit, ' North Indians: A Study of their Economic, Social and Political Activities with Special Reference to Selangor, 1870s-1940s '. See 265

1492. Jackson, R. N., *Immigrant Labour and the Development of Malaya 1786-1920* See 373

1493. Jagatheesan, N., ' Immigration of Indian Labour into Malaya, 1867-1910 ' See 375

1494. Jain, Ravindra K., *Migrants, Proletarians or Malayan?—South Indians on the Plantation Frontier in Malaya* See 379

1495. *Ramanathapuram Experiment: Paradigm of An Estate-farm-factory Community in Malaya* See 380

1496. *South Indians on the Plantation Frontier in Malaya* See 381

1497. James, A. Ongkili, *Modernizatitn in East Malaysia 1960-1970* (Kuala Lumpur- Oxford University Press, 1974)

1498. James, A. Palmore, Ramesh Chandra and Z. Fernandez Dorothy, ' The Demographic Situation in Malaysia ' in John F. Kanther and Lee Mccaffrey (eds.), *Population and Development in South-East Asia* (Honolulu: East-West Population Institute, 1975)

1499. Jegadeva, Kularatnam, ' Indian Immigration into Malaya, 1910-1941 ' Thesis Submitted for the Degree of Bachelor of Arts, University of Malaya, Singapore, 1959

1500. Kasper, Wolfgang, *Malayasia: A Study in Successful Economic Development* See 378

1501. Khan, Latiffa. ' Indians in Malaya, 1900-1945 ' Thesis Submitted for the Degree of Master of Arts, University of Hong Kong, Hong Kong, 1963

1502. Kratoska, Paul H., ' The Chettiar and the Yeoman—British Cultural Categories and Rural Indebtedness in Malaya ' See 578

1503. Krishnan, R. B., *Indians in Malaya: A Peageant of Greater India* (Singapore: The Author, 1936)

1504. Lee, Yong Leng, ' Population Changes in Sabah, 1951-1960 ' See 172

1505. Lim, Chong-Yoh, *Population: In his Economic Development of Modern Malaya* See 173

1506. Lim, David, *Economic Growth and Development in West Malaysia* See 392

1507. Lim, Tech Ghee, *Peasants and their Agricultural Economy in Colonial Malaya* 1874-1941 See 393

1508. Ma, Ronald, and Yoh Poh Seng, ' The Economic Characteris-stics of the Population of the Federation of Malaya, 1957 ' See 395

1509. MacGregor, R. B., *Reports on the Registration of Births and Deaths for the Year* 1947 (Kuala Lumpur: Government Press, 1948)

1510. Mahadevan, Raman, ' Pattern of Enterprise of Immigrant Entrepreneurs—A study of Chettiars in Malaya ' See 266

1511. ———, ' Pattern of Enterprise of Immigrant Entrepreneurs—A Study of Chettiars in Malaya ' See 267

1512. Mahajani, Usha, *The Role of Indian Minorities in Burma and Malaya* See 1199

1513. Marjoribanks, N. E., ond A. K. G. Ahmad Tambi Marakkayar, *Report on Indian Labour Emigrating to Ceylon and Malaya* See 401

1514. McGee Terence Gurry, ' Population: A Preliminary Analysis ' See 174

1515. McNair, J. F. A., *Perak, and the Malaya* (London: Tinsley, 1876)

1516. McTraggart, W. Donald, ' The Distribution of Ethnic Groups in Malaya, 1947-1957 ' See 269

1517. McTaggart, W. Donald and Duane Stormont, *Mapping Ethnic Groups in Malayasia* See 270

1518. Mills, L. A., *Malaya: A Political and Economic Appraisal* See 406

1519. Mills, Lennox A., *British Rule In Eastern Asia: A Study of Contemporary Government and Economic Development in British Malaya and Hong Kong* (London: Oxford University Press, 1942)

1520. Mohammad, Ibrahim Ahmad Bin, *Towards a History of Law in Malaysia and Singapore* (Singapore: Standford College Press, 1970)

1521. Moothedan, A. Varkey, *Our Countrymen in Malaya: Being a Review of the Social, Economic and Political Position of Indians in Malaya* See 272

1522. Nair, N. M., *Indians in Malaya* (Koduvayur: The Koduvayur Printing Works, 1937)

1523. Nanjundan, S., *Indians in the Malayan Economy* See 415

1524. Narayanaswamy, K., *Proses Assimilasi dan Pengebudayaan Di-Kalangan Masharakat Chitty Melaka* (Kuala Lumpur; University of Malaya, 1968)

1525. Nathan, J. E., *The Census of British Malaya* 1921 (London: Waterlow, 1922)

1526. Netto, George, *Indians in Malaya: Historical Facts and Figures* See 219

1527. A Note on 'Indians in Overseas-Malaya: Chettiars in Malaya' *The Indian Review* (Madras) Vol. 50. No. 11. November 1949

1528. A Note on 'Indians Outside India—Malaya' *The Indian Review* (Madras) Vol. 57, No. 1 January 1956

1529. Office of the Economic Adviser, India, *Indians in Malayan Economy* See 423

1530. Ooi, Jin-bee, 'Rural Development in Tropical Areas with Special Reference to Malaya' See 424

1531. ———, *Land, People and Economy in Malaya* See 125

1532. *A Petition of Nattukottai Chettiars of Malaya to His Excellency Admiral Lord Louis Mountbatten, Supreme Allied Commander, South East Asian Command, Singapore*, 1945. This document is part of a large collection of official papers of the Burma Nattukottai Chettiar Association, Rangoon

1533. Poutney, A. M., *The Census of the Federated Malay States 1911* See 175

1534. Puthucheary, James, *Ownership and Control in the Malayan Economy* See 434

1535. Rabeendran, R., *Ethno-racial Marginality in West Malaysia: The Case of the Peranakan Hindu Melaka or Malacca Chitty Community* See 279

1536. Raghavan, N., *India and Malaya* (London: Orient Longmans, 1954)

1537. Rajeswari, A, 'Tamil Journalism and the Indian Community in Malaya 1920-1941' See 582

1538. Ramachandran, G. P., *The Indian Independence Movement in Malaya 1942-1945* (Kuala Lumpur: University of Malaya: 1970)

1539. *Report of the Commission on Conditions of Indentured Labour* See 478

1540. *Report of the Commission on Conditions of Indentured Labour* See 479

1541. *Report of the Brigadier-General Sir Samuel Wilson Under Secretary of State for the Colonies on his Visit to Malaya* Cmd. 4276, Kuala Lumpur, 1932

1542. *A Report on the* 1947 *Census of Population—Malaya* (London, 1949)

1543. Robequain, Charles (Translatec by E. D. Laborde) *Malaya, Indonesia, Borneo and the Philippines* (London: Longmans Green, 1954)

1544. Ryan, N. J., *A History of Malaysia and Singapore* See 227

1545. Sandhu, Kernial Singh, 'Indian Migration and Population Change in Malaya, c. 100-1957 A.D.: A Historical Geography' See 177

1546. ———, ' Some Preliminary Observations of Origins and the Characteristics of Indian Migration to Malaya, 1776-1957 ' See 178

1547. ———, *Indians in Malaya: Immigration and Settlement 1786-1957* (London: Cambridge University Press, 1969)

1548. ———, *Early Malaysia* (Singapore: University Education Press, 1973)

1549. Sastri, C. Siva Rama, ' Communism in Malaysia ' *Modern Review* (Calcutta) Vol. LXXXIV, No. 2, 1948

1550. Saw, Swee-Hock and Cheng, Soik-Hwa. *A Bibliography of the Demography of Malaysia and Burnei* (Singapore: University Education Press, 1975)

1551. Saw, Swee-Hock and Pearl Chu, 'The Population of Nineteenth Century Penang' See 179
1552. Selvaratnam, V., 'Indian Plantation Workers in West Malaysia' See 491
1553. Shantakumar, G., 'A Note on Projection of Populations of National and Sub-national Areas in Malaya'. See 181
1554. Sidhu, Manjit Singh, *Kuala Lumpur and Its Population* (Kuala Lumpur: Surinder Publications, 1978)
1555. S. K. D., *Nattukkottai Chettiars in Malaya* (Singapore: Kiat, 1958) Pamphlet reproducing articles from the *Malayan Law Journal*
1556. Smith, T. E., *Population Growth in Malaya* See 182
1557. *Social Statistics Bulletin, Peninsular Malaysia,* 1972 (Kuala Lumpur: Department of Statistics, 1975)
1558. *Some Implications of Rapid Population Growth in Peninsular Malaysia* See 183
1559. South Indian Labour Fund Board, *Kuala Lumpur* (Annual Report, 1961) (Kuala Lumpur: Jabatan Chetak Kerajaan, 1962)
1560. *Statistical Hand Book, Sabah,* 1974 (Kuala Lumpur: Department of Statistics, 1975)
1561. *Statistical Hand Book of Peninsular Malaysia,* 1975 (Kuala Lumpur: Department of Statistics, 1976)
1562. *Statistical Hand Book, Sarawak,* 1975 (Kuching: Department of Statistics, 1976)
1563. Straits Settlements. *Office of the Honorary Commissioner for Depressed Classes, Straits Settlements and Federated Malaya States—Reports* (Chidambaram: Karthikeyan Press, 1926-1928)
1564. Subbiah, Rama. *Tamil Malaysians: a Checklist of Tamil Books and Periodicals Published in Malaysia and Singapore* (Kuala Lumpur: University of Malaya Library, 1969)
1565. Subramaniam, S. 'Politics of the Indians in Malaya 1945-1955 Kuala Lumpur' M. A. Thesis University of Malaya, Kuala Lumpur, 1973
1566. *Third Malaysian Plan, 1976-1980* (Kuala Lumpur: Director General of Printing, 1976)

1567. Thomson, F. A., ' The Impact of Culture on Birth Rate and Population Increase in the Federation of Malaya' See 185
1568. Thompson, Virginia, *Postmortem on Malaya* (New York: Macmillan, 1943)
1569. Verhoeven, F. R. J., ' Some Notes on the History of the Tamil Country in Dutch Malacca (1641-1825) ' See 240
1570. *Vital Statistics: Peninsular Malaysia*, 1974 (Kuala Lumpur: Department of Statistics, 1976)
1571. Vlieland, C. A., *British Malaya: A Report on the* 1931 *Census and on Certain Problems of Vital Statistics* See 179
1572. ———, ' The Population of the Malay Peninsula ' See 188
1573. ———, ' The 1947 Census of Malaya ' See 189
1574. Wiebe, Paul D. and S. Mariappan, ' Ethnic Insularity and National Identification in a Plural Society: Indian Malaysians—A Case Study ' See 290
1575. Winstedt, R. O., *The Malaysian Cultural History* See 242
1576. ———, *A History of Malaya* (Singapore: Maricor and Sons, 1962)
1577. *Women Today in Peninsular Malaysia* (Kuala Lumpur: The Federation of Family Planning Associations, 1976)
1578. Wong, David, S. Y. *Tenure and Land Dealings in the Malay States* See 519
1579. You, Pop Seng, ' The Population of Malaya ' See 190
1580. Zakaria, Abdul Aziz, *An Introduction to the Machinery of Government in Malaysia* (Kuala Lumpur: Dewan Bahasa Dan Pustaka, 1974)

## 16. NAGARATHARS IN SINGAPORE

1581. Arasaratnam, S., *Indians in Malaysia and Singapore* See 1448
1582. Braddell, Roland, *The Light of Singapore* (London: Methuen, 1947)
1583. Challis, Joyce, *Annotated Bibliography of Economic and Social Material in Singapore and West Malaysia* See 322
1584. Jumabhoy, R., *Multiracial Singapore* See 264
1585. Kassim, Ismail, ' The Chettiars ' See 48
1586. ———, ' The Chettiar—Is He A Vanishing Breed?' *New Notation* (Singapore) 25 November 1975
1587. Mani, A., ' Caste Among Singapore Hindus ' See 268
1588. Mohammad, Ibrahim Ahmad Bin, *Towards a History of Law in Malaysia and Singapore* See 1520
1589. Muthusamy, Damayanthi, *Sri Thandayudapani Temple*, Singapore See 538
1590. Sandhu, Kernial Singh, ' Some Aspects of Indian Settlement in Singapore' *Journal of South-East Asian History* (Singapore) Vol. 10, 2 September 1969
1591. Saw, Swee Hock, *Singapore Populatin in Transition* (Philadelphia: University of Pennsylvania Press, 1970)
1592. Saw, Swee Hock and Cheng Soik-Hwa. *A Bibliography of the Demography of Singapore* (Singapore: University Education Press, 1975)
1593. *Singapore Hindus' Religious and Culturcl Seminar* 1969-1971 See 550
1594. *Singapore Street Directory and Guide* (Singapore: Singapore Survey Department, 1954)
1595. 'Straits Settlements: Indian Immigration Agent' *Annual Reports* 1890-1906 Singapore 1891-1907 (Continued as Reports of Superintendent of Immigrants and subsequently Immigration Officer)
1596. Subbiah, Rama. *Tamil Malaysians: a Checklist of Tamil Books and Periodicals Published in Malaysia and Singapore* See 1564

## 17. NAGARATHARS IN VIETNAM AND OTHER COUNTRIES

1597. Angangco, Ofelia Regale, ' The Indian Community in the Philippines ' See 245

1598. Benedict, Burson, *Indians in a Plural Society : Report on Mauritius* See 15

1599. Coédes, Genge, *Les etats Hindouises et d Indonesia* See 23

1600. Lamb, Helen, B., *Studies on India and Vietnam* See 53

1601. Robequain, Charles, (Translated by E. D. Laborde) *Malaya : Indonesia, Borneo and the Philippines* See 1543

# INDEX

The following Index is limited to the Introductory Essay up to page 52. There is no index for the bibliography as the entries are already in alphabetical order.

L



M



N



O



P